CEFR **B1+**

Live Escalate

Summit

Teruhiko Kadoyama

Live ABC editors

JN061731

SEIBIDO   LiveABC

Book **3**

photographs

iStockphoto

StreamLine

Web 動画・音声ファイルのストリーミング再生について

CD マーク及び Web 動画マークがある箇所は、PC、スマートフォン、タブレット端末において、無料でストリーミング再生することができます。下記 URL よりご利用ください。再生手順や動作環境などは本書巻末の「Web 動画のご案内」をご覧ください。

http://st.seibido.co.jp

音声ファイルのダウンロードについて

CD マークがある箇所は、ダウンロードすることも可能です。下記 URL の書籍詳細ページにあるダウンロードアイコンをクリックしてください。

http://seibido.co.jp/ad636

Live Escalate Book 3: Summit

Contents

Content Chart 04

Learning Overview 06

UNIT 01 **Electronic Devices** 10

UNIT 02 **Health and Fitness** 20

UNIT 03 **On the Phone** 30

UNIT 04 **Household Chores** 40

UNIT 05 **Environmental Protection** 50

UNIT 06 **Bargaining for Fun** 60

REVIEW 1 **Review 1** 70

UNIT 07 **Affinity** 74

UNIT 08 **Culture Shock** 84

UNIT 09 **School Activities** 94

UNIT 10 **Asking for Directions** 104

UNIT 11 **Tourist Spots** 114

UNIT 12 **Studying Abroad** 124

REVIEW 2 **Review 2** 134

LINGUAPORTA 138

StreamLine 139

CONTENT CHART

UNIT	COMMUNICATION STRATEGY	CONVERSATION
UNIT 01 **Electronic Devices**	• Learning the name of computer-related terms and discussing a recent Internet trend: the selfie	Communication Breakdown
UNIT 02 **Health and Fitness**	• Providing ways to keep healthy and stay fit	Living a Healthier Lifestyle
UNIT 03 **On the Phone**	• Introducing telephone etiquette • Practicing phone English	Calling a Customer Support Center
UNIT 04 **Household Chores**	• Discussing gender and household chores	Trading Places
UNIT 05 **Environmental Protection**	• Talking about the environment	Clean up Your Act by Recycling
UNIT 06 **Bargaining for Fun**	• Introducing useful tips for bargaining • Providing practical sentence patterns for bargaining	Snappy Shopper
REVIEW 1 **Review 1**		
UNIT 07 **Affinity**	• Introducing how different animal fathers take care of their young • Discussing parents' attitudes toward their children	A Father's Lessons
UNIT 08 **Culture Shock**	• Talking about tipping culture • Introducing some travel etiquette	Don't Forget the Tip!
UNIT 09 **School Activities**	• Introducing school clubs • Talking about the benefits of being a student	The Benefits of Being a Student
UNIT 10 **Asking for Directions**	• Practicing directions • Providing practical sentence patterns for asking directions	How Can We Get There?
UNIT 11 **Tourist Spots**	• Making travel plans • Introducing famous mountains around the world	Deciding on a Tour
UNIT 12 **Studying Abroad**	• Introducing homestay etiquette • Talking about the benefits of a homestay	A Welcome Dinner
REVIEW 2 **Review 2**		

GRAMMAR	READING	WRITING
• Present Perfect	Put Yourself in the Frame	Writing about your favorite app
• Factual and Unreal Conditionals	Daily Routines for Staying Fit	Creating a wellness plan
• Relative Adverbs	Tips for Speaking on the Telephone	Leaving a message for someone
• Passive Voice	Gender and Household Chores	Writing a passage based on pictures and prompts
• Indirect Questions	One Small Step Toward a Cleaner Planet	Writing a passage based on pictures and prompts
• Adverbial Clauses	Discounts and Deals	Writing a passage based on a sample article
• Causative Verbs • Inverted Sentences	Fathers in the Animal Kingdom	Making an invitation card
• Double Comparatives	Tips on Travel Etiquette	Making a list of dos and don'ts
• Tag Questions • Inverted Sentences	Join the Club!	Writing a passage based on a sample article
• Participle Phrases • Participle Construction	Keeping from Getting Lost	Writing a passage based on pictures
• Exclamatory Sentences • On/Upon + N./V-ing, S. + V. • It is said that …	Monuments to Love	Writing about your hometown
• Conjunctive Adverbs	Homestay Etiquette	Writing about your ideal homestay host

LEARNING OVERVIEW

The Live Escalate series comes in three volumes, from Book 1: Base Camp to Book 3: Summit. Each book is made up of 12 units and a review section after every six units. The following is the introduction for Book 3: Summit. There are reading, listening, writing, and speaking activities in each unit. Readers will be challenged by the variety of fun and interesting content throughout the series.

WARM UP

A warm-up section of the theme topic

Students start each lesson with critical-thinking questions. These thought-provoking questions will spark students' interest in the topic while also providing excellent speaking practice.

Students will strengthen their listening and speaking ability with these engaging activities. First is a listening comprehension quiz, which consists of some short dialogues or monologues. Next is a short role-play. Here, students will put their communication skills to the test in various real-life scenarios.

CONVERSATION

A dialogue about the theme topic with a variety of questions

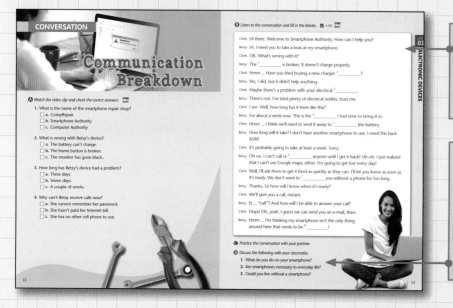

The dialogues use realistic, modern English to deliver practical and fun conversation practice.

Here, students will find various types of activities that will assess their understanding. Completing these tasks will help students feel confident in their English ability.

GRAMMAR
Explicit and lively grammar instruction through visuals

In this section, further information related to the grammar lesson is provided. The design, which resembles an instant-messaging service, is fun and relatable for students. They will feel like they have their own personal online tutor!

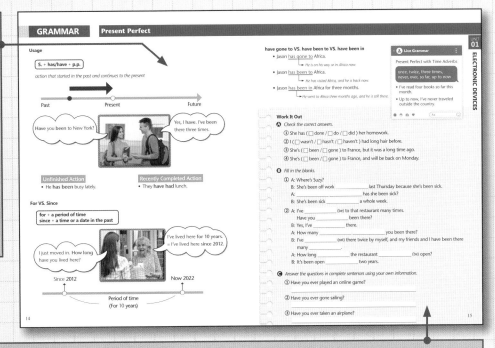

This quick and effective quiz provides students an instant assessment of what they've just learned. It also teaches them how and when to use the grammar points taught previously.

READING
An article about the theme topic with a variety of questions

The article features compelling topics and is filled with fascinating facts and information.

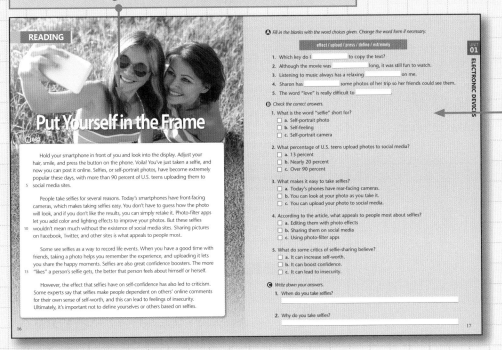

Students will check their comprehension with different types of review questions.

LEARNING OVERVIEW

WRITING

Have you ever played an interesting game? Look at the pictures and the sample article. Write about your favorite app. Share it with the class.

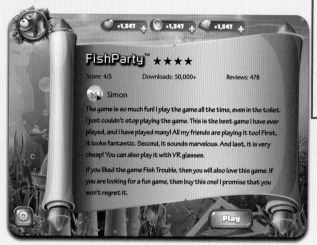

FishParty™ ★★★★

Score: 4/5   Downloads: 50,000+   Reviews: 478

Simon

The game is so much fun! I play the game all the time, even in the toilet. I just couldn't stop playing the game. This is the best game I have ever played, and I have played many! All my friends are playing it too! First, it looks fantastic. Second, it sounds marvelous. And last, it is very cheap! You can also play it with VR glasses.

If you liked the game Fish Trouble, then you will also love this game. If you are looking for a fun game, then buy this one! I promise that you won't regret it.

Play

WRITING

Real-life writing tasks, such as letters and essays

Useful sentence patterns and instructions are given to prompt students and get them started. Students will improve their writing skills while having fun along the way!

CHALLENGE YOURSELF

A topic-related listening test

This section provides an excellent tool for students to track their improvement and be aware of the improvement in their English proficiency.

CHALLENGE YOURSELF

Part I Question & Response 🎧 1-05

Listen to the statement or question and choose the best response.

1. ☐ a   ☐ b   ☐ c   4. ☐ a   ☐ b   ☐ c
2. ☐ a   ☐ b   ☐ c   5. ☐ a   ☐ b   ☐ c
3. ☐ a   ☐ b   ☐ c

Part II Conversations 🎧 1-06

Listen to the conversation and answer the questions.

6. What is true about the prize money?
   ☐ a. It's given out to only five people.
   ☐ b. It's the same for every person.
   ☐ c. It's based on how many people play.
   ☐ d. It's less than 25 dollars.

7. What is David going to do?
   ☐ a. Fix the woman's laptop
   ☐ b. Buy the woman a new laptop
   ☐ c. Ask the woman for a favor
   ☐ d. Take the woman on a date

8. What did the man do?
   ☐ a. He damaged the woman's computer.
   ☐ b. He got rid of the virus.
   ☐ c. He deleted the woman's hard drive.
   ☐ d. He bought a new computer.

9. What does the woman use more these days?
   ☐ a. Her tablet
   ☐ b. Her laptop
   ☐ c. The anti-virus program
   ☐ d. Her case

10. What's wrong with the man's computer?
   ☐ a. The webcam can't record.
   ☐ b. It has a virus.
   ☐ c. The mouse isn't working.
   ☐ d. The keyboard is gone.

Linguaporta Training

Let's review the unit with Linguaporta.

19

WELCOME TO *LIVE ESCALATE*!

The Live Escalate series comes in three volumes, from Book 1: Base Camp to Book 3: Summit. Each book is made up of 12 units and a review section after every six units. There are reading, listening, writing, and speaking activities in each unit. Readers will be challenged by the variety of fun and interesting content throughout the series.

A Complete Series

Each of the three books in this stimulating and pragmatic series is designed with a natural flow in mind: listening ⇨ speaking ⇨ reading ⇨ writing, with the result being that your English improves dramatically while you're unaware of the effort you've spent. The aim is that with minimal friction, learners of all ages will assimilate this language with the same fluidity a child does in his or her native environment, thus removing the sense of foreignness and frustration that is part of foreign language learning.

Unit Themes Focusing on Self-Expression

The units covered in this series pertain to ordinary life, focusing on the types of situations and challenges learners encounter every day, including shopping, eating, socializing, odds and ends around the house, leisure, and more.

Book 3: Summit
I CAN express opinions on some matters in a controlled way.

Book 2: Trekking
I CAN express opinions in a controlled way.

Book 1: Base Camp
I CAN take part in a conversation on a familiar topic.

Electronic Devices

TALK ABOUT THIS

Talk about these questions.

How often do you use a smartphone?

GEAR UP

A *Listen to the conversations and choose the correct pictures.* 🎧 1-02

Question 1.

Question 2.

Why do you think people take selfies?

B *Role-play with a partner. Extend the conversation as much as you can.*

Ⓐ What's wrong with the _____?

Ⓑ It's broken.

Ⓐ How long has it been broken?

Ⓑ It's been broken for _____.

Ⓐ Why don't you take it to _____?

Ⓑ Good idea. I'll take it this afternoon.

Question 3.

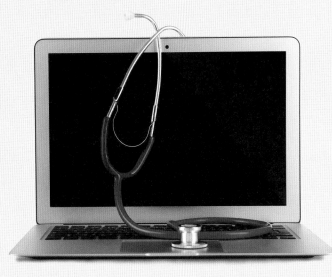

Communication Breakdown

A *Watch the video clip and check the correct answers.* 🖥️ WEB動画

1. What is the name of the smartphone repair shop?
   - ☐ **a.** CompRepair
   - ☐ **b.** Smartphone Authority
   - ☐ **c.** Computer Authority

2. What is wrong with Betsy's device?
   - ☐ **a.** The battery can't charge.
   - ☐ **b.** The home button is broken.
   - ☐ **c.** The monitor has gone black.

3. How long has Betsy's device had a problem?
   - ☐ **a.** Three days
   - ☐ **b.** Seven days
   - ☐ **c.** A couple of weeks

4. Why can't Betsy receive calls now?
   - ☐ **a.** She cannot remember her password.
   - ☐ **b.** She hasn't paid her Internet bill.
   - ☐ **c.** She has no other cell phone to use.

B *Listen to the conversation and fill in the blanks.* 🎧 1-03 📺

Clerk: Hi there. Welcome to Smartphone Authority. How can I help you?

Betsy: Hi. I need you to take a look at my smartphone.

Clerk: OK. What's wrong with it?

Betsy: The ^{1}_____ is broken. It doesn't charge properly.

Clerk: Hmm ... Have you tried buying a new charger ^{2}_____?

Betsy: Yes, I did, but it didn't help anything.

Clerk: Maybe there's a problem with your electrical ^{3}_____.

Betsy: There's not. I've tried plenty of electrical outlets, trust me.

Clerk: I see. Well, how long has it been like this?

Betsy: For about a week now. This is the ^{4}_____ I had time to bring it in.

Clerk: Hmm ... I think we'll need to send it away to ^{5}_____ the battery.

Betsy: How long will it take? I don't have another smartphone to use. I need this back ASAP.

Clerk: It's probably going to take at least a week. Sorry.

Betsy: Oh no. I can't call or ^{6}_____ anyone until I get it back! Uh-oh. I just realized that I can't use Google maps, either. I'm going to get lost every day!

Clerk: Well, I'll ask them to get it fixed as quickly as they can. I'll let you know as soon as it's ready. We don't want to ^{7}_____ you without a phone for too long.

Betsy: Thanks. So how will I know when it's ready?

Clerk: We'll give you a call, ma'am.

Betsy: Er ... "call"? And how will I be able to answer your call?

Clerk: Oops! Oh, yeah. I guess we can send you an e-mail, then.

Betsy: Hmm ... I'm thinking my smartphone isn't the only thing around here that needs to be ^{8}_____!

C *Practice the conversation with your partner.*

DISCUSSION

D *Discuss the following with your classmates.*

1. What do you do on your smartphone?
2. Are smartphones necessary to everyday life?
3. Could you live without a smartphone?

Usage

S. + has/have + p.p.

action that started in the past and continues to the present

Past   Present   Future

> **Have** you **been** to New York?

> Yes, I **have**. I've **been** there three times.

Unfinished Action
• He **has been** busy lately.

Recently Completed Action
• They **have had** lunch.

For VS. Since

for + a period of time
since + a time or a date in the past

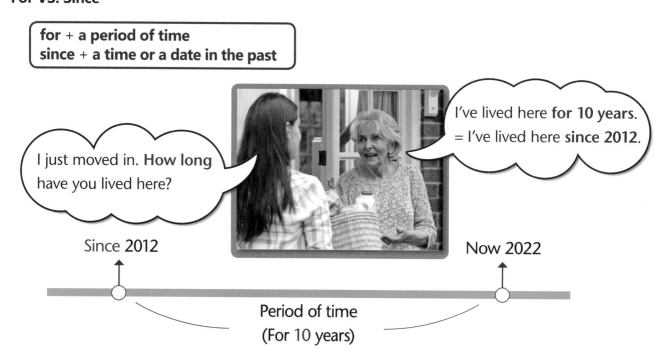

> I just moved in. **How long** have you lived here?

> I've lived here **for 10 years**.
> = I've lived here **since 2012**.

Since 2012   Now 2022

Period of time
(For 10 years)

have gone to VS. have been to VS. have been in

- Jason <u>has gone to</u> Africa.
  - ↳ *He is on his way or in Africa now.*
- Jason <u>has been to</u> Africa.
  - ↳ *He has visited Africa, and he is back now.*
- Jason <u>has been in</u> Africa for three months.
  - ↳ *He went to Africa three months ago, and he is still there.*

← 👤 **Live Grammar** ⋮

Present Perfect with Time Adverbs

> once, twice, three times, never, ever, so far, up to now

- I've read four books so far this month.
- Up to now, I've never traveled outside the country.

➕ 🅜 📷 ❤   (Aa   ☺)

Work It Out

Ⓐ *Check the correct answers.*

① She has (☐ done / ☐ do / ☐ did) her homework.

② I (☐ wasn't / ☐ hasn't / ☐ haven't) had long hair before.

③ She's (☐ been / ☐ gone) to France, but it was a long time ago.

④ She's (☐ been / ☐ gone) to France, and will be back on Monday.

Ⓑ *Fill in the blanks.*

① A: Where's Suzy?

B: She's been off work _____ last Thursday because she's been sick.

A: _____ _____ has she been sick?

B: She's been sick _____ a whole week.

② A: I've _____ (be) to that restaurant many times.
Have you _____ been there?

B: Yes, I've _____ there.

A: How many _____ _____ you been there?

B: I've _____ (eat) there twice by myself, and my friends and I have been there many _____.

A: How long _____ the restaurant _____ (be) open?

B: It's been open _____ two years.

Ⓒ *Answer the questions in complete sentences using your own information.*

① Have you ever played an online game?

_____

② Have you ever gone sailing?

_____

③ Have you ever taken an airplane?

_____

Put Yourself in the Frame

🎧 1-04

Hold your smartphone in front of you and look into the display. Adjust your hair, smile, and press the button on the phone. Voila! You've just taken a selfie, and now you can post it online. Selfies, or self-portrait photos, have become extremely popular these days, with more than 90 percent of U.S. teens uploading them to
5 social media sites.

People take selfies for several reasons. Today's smartphones have front-facing cameras, which makes taking selfies easy. You don't have to guess how the photo will look, and if you don't like the results, you can simply retake it. Photo-filter apps let you add color and lighting effects to improve your photos. But these selfies
10 wouldn't mean much without the existence of social media sites. Sharing pictures on Facebook, Twitter, and other sites is what appeals to people most.

Some see selfies as a way to record life events. When you have a good time with friends, taking a photo helps you remember the experience, and uploading it lets you share the happy moments. Selfies are also great confidence boosters. The more
15 "likes" a person's selfie gets, the better that person feels about himself or herself.

However, the effect that selfies have on self-confidence has also led to criticism. Some experts say that selfies make people dependent on others' online comments for their own sense of self-worth, and this can lead to feelings of insecurity. Ultimately, it's important not to define yourselves or others based on selfies.

A *Fill in the blanks with the word choices given. Change the word form if necessary.*

effect / upload / press / define / extremely

1. Which key do I _____ to copy the text?

2. Although the movie was _____ long, it was still fun to watch.

3. Listening to music always has a relaxing _____ on me.

4. Sharon has _____ some photos of her trip so her friends could see them.

5. The word "love" is really difficult to _____.

B *Check the correct answers.*

1. What is the word "selfie" short for?
   - ☐ **a.** Self-portrait photo
   - ☐ **b.** Self-feeling
   - ☐ **c.** Self-portrait camera

2. What percentage of U.S. teens upload photos to social media?
   - ☐ **a.** 13 percent
   - ☐ **b.** Nearly 20 percent
   - ☐ **c.** Over 90 percent

3. What makes it easy to take selfies?
   - ☐ **a.** Today's phones have rear-facing cameras.
   - ☐ **b.** You can look at your photo as you take it.
   - ☐ **c.** You can upload your photo to social media.

4. According to the article, what appeals to people most about selfies?
   - ☐ **a.** Editing them with photo effects
   - ☐ **b.** Sharing them on social media
   - ☐ **c.** Using photo-filter apps

5. What do some critics of selfie-sharing believe?
   - ☐ **a.** It can increase self-worth.
   - ☐ **b.** It can boost confidence.
   - ☐ **c.** It can lead to insecurity.

C *Write down your answers.*

1. When do you take selfies?

   _____

2. Why do you take selfies?

   _____

WRITING

Have you ever played an interesting game? Look at the pictures and the sample article. Write about your favorite app. Share it with the class.

+1,547   **+1,547**   **+1,547**

FishParty™ ★★★★

Score: 4/5   Downloads: 50,000+   Reviews: 478

Simon

The game is so much fun! I play the game all the time, even in the toilet. I just couldn't stop playing the game. This is the best game I have ever played, and I have played many! All my friends are playing it too! First, it looks fantastic. Second, it sounds marvelous. And last, it is very cheap! You can also play it with VR glasses.

If you liked the game Fish Trouble, then you will also love this game. If you are looking for a fun game, then buy this one! I promise that you won't regret it.

Play

CHALLENGE YOURSELF

Part I Question & Response 🎧 1-05

Listen to the statement or question and choose the best response.

1. ☐ a ☐ b ☐ c
2. ☐ a ☐ b ☐ c
3. ☐ a ☐ b ☐ c

4. ☐ a ☐ b ☐ c
5. ☐ a ☐ b ☐ c

Part II Conversations 🎧 1-06

Listen to the conversation and answer the questions.

6. What is true about the prize money?
   ☐ a. It's given out to only five people.
   ☐ b. It's the same for every person.
   ☐ c. It's based on how many people play.
   ☐ d. It's less than 25 dollars.

7. What is David going to do?
   ☐ a. Fix the woman's laptop
   ☐ b. Buy the woman a new laptop
   ☐ c. Ask the woman for a favor
   ☐ d. Take the woman on a date

8. What did the man do?
   ☐ a. He damaged the woman's computer.
   ☐ b. He got rid of the virus.
   ☐ c. He deleted the woman's hard drive.
   ☐ d. He bought a new computer.

9. What does the woman use more these days?
   ☐ a. Her tablet
   ☐ b. Her laptop
   ☐ c. The anti-virus program
   ☐ d. Her case

10. What's wrong with the man's computer?
   ☐ a. The webcam can't record.
   ☐ b. It has a virus.
   ☐ c. The mouse isn't working.
   ☐ d. The keyboard is gone.

Linguaporta Training

Let's review the unit with Linguaporta.

Health and Fitness

WARM UP

TALK ABOUT THIS

Talk about these questions.

> Have you ever lost weight by going on a diet or exercising often? Did it work?

GEAR UP

A *Listen to the short talks and choose the correct pictures.* 🎧 1-07

Question 1.

Question 2.

Do you have any good or bad health habits, like never staying up late or never eating vegetables? Share one of each with your classmates.

B *Role-play with a partner. Extend the conversation as much as you can.*

Ⓐ How often do you work out?

Ⓑ I work out <u>every day / once a week / two or three times a week</u>.

....

Ⓐ How many hours do you usually sleep every day?

Ⓑ I sleep at least _____ hours.

....

Ⓐ What do you usually do to relax?

Ⓑ I _____ to relax.

21

Living a Healthier Lifestyle

A *Watch the video clip and check the correct answers.* WEB動画

1. What is the conversation mainly about?
   - ☐ **a.** What restaurants to go to
   - ☐ **b.** Ways to avoid gaining weight
   - ☐ **c.** How to drink more soda

2. What is NOT mentioned in the conversation?
   - ☐ **a.** Cycling is good exercise.
   - ☐ **b.** Soda might make you fat.
   - ☐ **c.** Skipping meals is bad for you.

3. What can we say about the café?
   - ☐ **a.** It serves a lot of fast food that is very unhealthy.
   - ☐ **b.** It has very good prices for some types of coffee.
   - ☐ **c.** It's pretty close to where the man and woman are.

4. What is true about Frank?
   - ☐ **a.** He drank one can of soda last night.
   - ☐ **b.** He is extremely hungry.
   - ☐ **c.** He had a big breakfast this morning.

B *Listen to the conversation and fill in the blanks.* 🔘 1-08 🖥️

Emma: What are you going to eat for lunch?

Frank: I'm not sure. But I'm going to eat a lot.

Emma: Why?

Frank: I ¹_____ too much coffee last night. I woke up late, so I didn't have time for breakfast. Now I'm really hungry.

Emma: You should be careful. I read that if you often ²_____ breakfast, you might eat too much for lunch and gain weight.

Frank: But I'm ³_____!

Emma: I know. I'm just trying to help. A lot of people say that students ⁴_____ weight in their first year of college.

Frank: All right. Do you have any other ⁵_____ for me?

Emma: Maybe you shouldn't drink so much soda. It can make you fat.

Frank: OK, I'll keep that in mind. Thanks. I'm going to ⁶_____ to a fast-food restaurant now.

Emma: What? Why don't you just walk over to the café? It's only a 15-minute walk, and they have ⁷_____ food.

Frank: Oh, yeah. I guess you are right. The café's not far, either.

Emma: Plus, you'll get some exercise on the way there.

Frank: And now I'm so hungry, I ⁸_____ run all the way there.

C *Practice the conversation with your partner.*

DISCUSSION

D *Discuss the following with your classmates.*

1. What can you do to live a healthier life?
2. Is it OK to eat fast food once a week? Why?
3. Do you do any exercise? What kind?

Zero Conditional

We use zero conditional to describe things that are always true or scientific facts.

If + present simple, S. + present simple

If you heat ice, it melts.

- If I **come** home late, my parents **get** angry.

First Conditional

We use first conditional to describe a possible situation in the future.

If + present simple, S. + future tense (will + V.)

- If it **rains**, I **will stay** home.
- If Jerry **finishes** his homework, He **will play** video games.

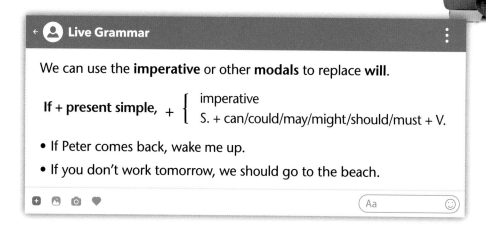

← 👤 **Live Grammar**   ⋮

We can use the **imperative** or other **modals** to replace **will**.

If + present simple, + { imperative
S. + can/could/may/might/should/must + V.

- If Peter comes back, wake me up.
- If you don't work tomorrow, we should go to the beach.

➕ 🖼 📷 ♥   (Aa   ☺)

Second Conditional

We use second conditional to describe imaginary or unlikely situations in the present or future.

If + past simple, S. + would/should/could/might + V.

- If you **went** to bed earlier, you **wouldn't be** so tired.
- If the hat **were** red, I **wouldn't buy** it.

Third Conditional

We use third conditional to describe an imaginary situation that did not happen; often used to express regret or mistake.

> If + past perfect, S. + would/should/could/might + have + p.p.

- If you **had studied** harder, you **would have passed** the exam.
- If Dan **had told** me to bring an umbrella, I **wouldn't have gotten** wet.

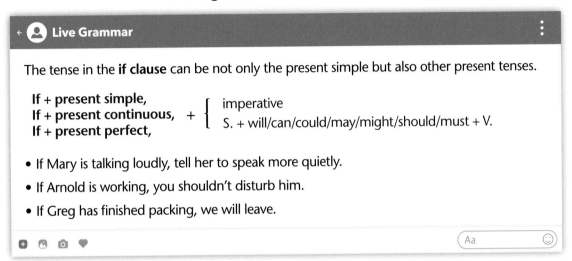

← 👤 **Live Grammar**   ⋮

The tense in the **if clause** can be not only the present simple but also other present tenses.

If + present simple,
If + present continuous, + { imperative
If + present perfect,   S. + will/can/could/may/might/should/must + V.

- If Mary is talking loudly, tell her to speak more quietly.
- If Arnold is working, you shouldn't disturb him.
- If Greg has finished packing, we will leave.

➕ 🅰 📷 ♥   (Aa)   ☺

Work It Out

Ⓐ *Complete the following sentences using the correct form.*

① If Frank _____ (go to the library), he studies for hours.

② If you _____ (stop at the store), pick up some milk.

③ If you _____ (not hurry), we will miss the train.

④ If Joan _____ (study hard), she could get better grades.

⑤ If I _____ (have enough money then), I could have gone abroad.

Ⓑ *Combine the two sentences using if.*

① John comes back today. / Tell him I called.

_____

② I had a car of my own. / I could drive it to work.

_____

③ Chris has seen that movie already. / We'll go and see a different one.

_____

DAILY ROUTINES FOR STAYING FIT

🎧CD 1-09

To stay in shape, many people work up a sweat in gyms and sometimes even skip meals. But did you know a fit body can be achieved just by changing a few habits? With these tips, you can burn hundreds of calories daily without even trying.

Fuel Your Day

5 Eat a healthy breakfast. When you're asleep at night, your body is fasting. Eating breakfast tells your body that you're not hungry. As a result, your body burns fat even when you're performing normal activities.

Light and Frequent Meals

Eat in small amounts every few hours. This lets your body use more energy to digest
10 food than eating three large meals a day does.

Drink Water

Drinking water increases the rate at which you burn calories. Scientists in Germany found that drinking at least 1.5 liters of water daily over a year can result in the loss of around 2.5 kilograms.

15 ## Do Housework

Cleaning the house may not sound like fun, but it provides just as good a workout as spending hours at the gym does. Thirty minutes of sweeping can take off almost a hundred calories!

Climb and Stand

20 If you want to stay fit, take the stairs. Five minutes of stair climbing burns around 150 calories. Also, your body burns fat more effectively when you're standing. Choose to stand rather than sit and you could be burning many extra calories every day.

Sleep More

Experts say that sleeping soundly for eight hours can get rid of 360 calories. If you don't
25 have time for the gym, there's no need to stress. Some small changes to your daily routine may be all that you need to get fit.

A *Fill in the blanks with the word choices given. Change the word form if necessary.*

energy / achieve / increase / get rid of / perform

1. You can _____ your dreams if you work hard and take chances.

2. The students _____ a play for the school yesterday.

3. For the past month I've been spending all my time and _____ on trying to find a job.

4. Food prices have _____ over the past few months.

5. You should _____ that old coat if you don't wear it anymore.

B *Check the correct answers.*

1. How often does the article recommend you eat?
   - ☐ **a.** Every few hours
   - ☐ **b.** Three times a day
   - ☐ **c.** Only twice a day

2. How can drinking water help you lose weight?
   - ☐ **a.** It increases the rate at which you burn calories.
   - ☐ **b.** It increases the rate at which you digest food.
   - ☐ **c.** It tells your body that you're not hungry.

3. Which of the following is NOT recommended by the article?
   - ☐ **a.** Sleeping eight hours every night
   - ☐ **b.** Cleaning your house
   - ☐ **c.** Sitting rather than standing

4. How many calories can you burn with five minutes of stair climbing?
   - ☐ **a.** Around 150
   - ☐ **b.** Roughly 250
   - ☐ **c.** About 360

5. Who might benefit from the exercise tips in this article?
   - ☐ **a.** Someone who loves going to the gym
   - ☐ **b.** Someone who doesn't want to lose weight
   - ☐ **c.** Someone who doesn't have enough time for the gym

C *Write down your answers.*

Do you have any tips on staying fit? Write them down and share with your partner.

_____

_____

_____

Read the following plan and write your own.

CREATE A WELLNESS PLAN

1. EVALUATE YOUR PHYSICAL WELLNESS
- I get tired during the afternoon.
- I have trouble lifting heavy things.
- I get exhausted when I walk up a lot of stairs.
- I ride my bike occasionally.

3. SET GOALS
- I want to have more energy.
- I'd like to focus on improving my cardio.
- I need to eat healthier: more vegetables and less junk food.
- I still want to eat pizza, but only once a month!

2. EVALUATE YOUR NUTRITIONAL WELLNESS
- I eat a lot of French fries and pizza for lunch at school.
- Sometimes I like to eat donuts for breakfast.
- I eat a lot of fruit, but I don't eat many vegetables.

4. WRITE A PARAGRAPH DESCRIBING YOUR PLAN
I'm going to exercise for 30 minutes at least five times a week. I'll also do body-weight exercises, like planks and push-ups, in order to improve my strength. A healthier diet, including fruits, vegetables, and lean meats, will help me feel better, have more energy, and get results.

CREATE A WELLNESS PLAN

1. EVALUATE YOUR PHYSICAL WELLNESS

3. SET GOALS

2. EVALUATE YOUR NUTRITIONAL WELLNESS

4. WRITE A PARAGRAPH DESCRIBING YOUR PLAN

28

CHALLENGE YOURSELF

Part I Question & Response 🎧 1-10

Listen to the statement or question and choose the best response.

1. ☐ a ☐ b ☐ c
2. ☐ a ☐ b ☐ c
3. ☐ a ☐ b ☐ c

4. ☐ a ☐ b ☐ c
5. ☐ a ☐ b ☐ c

Part II Conversations 🎧 1-11

Listen to the conversation and answer the questions.

6. What does the woman like to do before she goes to work?
   ☐ a. She likes to work in her garden.
   ☐ b. She likes to sleep.
   ☐ c. She likes to exercise.
   ☐ d. She likes to make a healthy lunch.

7. What is the man going to do about dinner?
   ☐ a. Not eat dinner
   ☐ b. Eat dinner very quickly
   ☐ c. Eat a small dinner
   ☐ d. Eat fast food for dinner

8. What is the man going to do?
   ☐ a. Find out if it is true that fruit juice has a lot of calories
   ☐ b. Drink soda instead of fruit juice
   ☐ c. Stop drinking fruit juice that has a lot of calories
   ☐ d. Remember that fruit juice has a lot of calories

9. What does the woman think about pizza?
   ☐ a. It is not good for you.
   ☐ b. It is too expensive to eat all the time.
   ☐ c. It is very good for you.
   ☐ d. It is fun and easy to eat.

10. What does going to the gym do for the woman?
    ☐ a. It helps her meet single men.
    ☐ b. It makes her feel less worry and anxiety.
    ☐ c. It helps her to stay up late at night.
    ☐ d. It gives her something to do at night.

Linguaporta Training

Let's review the unit with Linguaporta.

On the Phone

WARM UP

TALK ABOUT THIS

Talk about these questions.

Do you have any good, bad, or special telephone conversation experiences? Share one with your classmates.

GEAR UP

A *Listen to the short talks and choose the correct pictures.* 🎵 1-12

Question 1.

Question 2.

Do you prefer text messaging or telephoning?

Question 3.

B *Role-play with a partner. Extend the conversation as much as you can.*

Ⓐ Hi, _____. How are you doing?

Ⓑ <u>Pretty good. / Not too bad.</u>

....

Ⓐ Hi, this is _____. I'd like to speak to _____, please.

Ⓑ I'm sorry. You have the wrong number.

....

Ⓐ Who's this?

Ⓑ It's _____. Can I speak to _____?

Ⓐ <u>He's / She's</u> not back yet.

Ⓑ I'll call back later.

Calling a Customer Support Center

A *Watch the video clip and check the correct answers.* WEB動画 🖥

1. What is the name of the billing department representative?
   - ☐ **a.** Ms. Jennings
   - ☐ **b.** Ted
   - ☐ **c.** It is not mentioned in the conversation.

2. What is Samantha's problem?
   - ☐ **a.** She thinks she was charged too much money.
   - ☐ **b.** She lost her phone bill.
   - ☐ **c.** She wants to buy an international data plan.

3. What do we know about Samantha's phone plan?
   - ☐ **a.** It does not allow for roaming charges.
   - ☐ **b.** It has an associated phone number that is five digits long.
   - ☐ **c.** It includes one gigabyte of data for international use.

4. Which of the following is true?
   - ☐ **a.** Samantha forgot that her international data plan is not unlimited.
   - ☐ **b.** The billing department representative didn't solve her problem.
   - ☐ **c.** Samantha was not satisfied with the customer service.

B *Listen to the conversation and fill in the blanks.* 🎧 1-13 📺

Samantha calls her cell phone company's customer support center.

CSR*: Thank you for calling Superior Mobile. This is Ted speaking. How may I help you?

Samantha: Hi, I have a question about my most recent phone ¹_____.

CSR: Of course, ma'am. May I have your name, please?

Samantha: My name is Samantha Jennings.

CSR: All right, Ms. Jennings. I will ²_____ you to our billing department. Please hold.

Samantha: Thank you.

BDR**: Thank you for waiting, Ms. Jennings. I've been informed that there is an ³_____ with your most recent phone bill. Is that correct?

Samantha: Yes, that's correct. I believe I've been ⁴_____.

BDR: All right. May I have your mobile number, please?

Samantha: Sure, it's 105-210-5555.

BDR: OK, Ms. Jennings, I have your information here. May I ask what specific charges you are ⁵_____ to?

Samantha: I've been ⁶_____ roaming charges. I did use my phone while traveling abroad, but I have an international data plan.

BDR: Well, you do indeed have an international data plan, but I'm afraid it's not an ⁷_____ plan. Only the first gigabyte of data is covered.

Samantha: Oh, that's right! I didn't remember that! OK, well, I guess that ⁸_____ it. That's all I needed to know. Thank you for your assistance.

BDR: Not at all. Thank you for calling, Ms. Jennings. Have a nice day.

Samantha: You too. Goodbye.

*CSR = Customer service representative   ***BDR = Billing department representative*

C *Practice the conversation with your partner.*

DISCUSSION

D *Discuss the following with your classmates.*

  1. What is an unlimited data plan?

  2. How much data do you use every day?

  3. What kinds of apps use the most data?

33

A relative adverb is an adverb that introduces an adjective clause. It is used to start a description for a noun.

Relative Adverb	Meaning	Use
when	in/on which	*time*
where	in/at which	*place*
why	for which	*reason*

- Do you remember <u>the day **when** I first met you</u>?
  N.   + Adj. clause

  = Do you remember the day **on which** I first met you?

- <u>The house **where** the Browns live</u> is next to the park.
  N.   + Adj. clause

  = The house **in which** the Browns live is next to the park.

- Please tell me <u>the reason **why** you didn't go to school today</u>.

  = Please tell me the reason **for which** you didn't go to school today.

← 👤 **Live Grammar**   ⋮

When a sentence has a relative adverb and a noun, the relative adverb can be deleted.

- Mandy will never forget the day Ray kissed her.
  → **when** *is deleted*

- I don't remember the place I left my ring.
  → **where** *is deleted*

- Do you know the reason Sarah is late?
  → **why** *is deleted*

➕ 🖼 📷 ♥   (Aa   ☺)

Work It Out

Ⓐ *Check the correct answers.*

① Do you know the hotel (☐ when / ☐ where / ☐ why) John is staying?

② I don't understand the reason (☐ when / ☐ where / ☐ why) you won't talk to Marco.

③ Next Thursday is the day (☐ when / ☐ where / ☐ why) Jim is leaving for New York.

④ This is the library from (☐ that / ☐ which / ☐ when) I borrowed those books.

⑤ The teacher wants to figure out the reason for (☐ why / ☐ that / ☐ which) the students all failed.

Ⓑ *Combine the two sentences based on the hints given.*

① ⌈ The dinner will be held somewhere.
  ⌊ Alan knows the place. (where)

Alan _____

② ⌈ I can never forget the day.
  ⌊ We first met on that day. (when)

I can _____

③ ⌈ My boyfriend was late for our date.
  ⌊ I don't know the reason. (why)

I don't know _____

④ ⌈ No one could remember the date.
  ⌊ Doug was born on that date. (when)

No one _____

⑤ ⌈ I lost my purse in the restaurant.
  ⌊ I'm going back to the restaurant. (in which)

I'm going _____

⑥ ⌈ He went to work in a factory.
  ⌊ In that factory, the men were tough and fought about everything. (where)

He went to work _____

Tips for Speaking on the Telephone

CD 1-14

Learning how to communicate in English isn't easy, that's for sure. It helps, however, to be able to see the person who is talking to us, so we can get clues as to what they're saying. Hands will often draw the thing they're talking about or point in the direction they're suggesting; eyes can show us their mood and a
5 little about their thoughts; and lips can help us see what words they're saying. But one situation where we can't get this communication aid is when talking on the phone.

Telephone conversations can be frightening for anyone if spoken in a language that is still being learned. But speaking a foreign language on the
10 phone can be a great tool for improving our listening and speaking ability. It's something we shouldn't avoid. In fact, we should seek out ways to have more conversations over the phone.

By not having any clues about what the other person is saying, we have to rely on listening ability alone. It's a little difficult at first, for sure, but we will
15 find our listening comprehension improving dramatically the more telephone conversations we have. We can learn some cool phrases that are unique to telephone talk too. It's like somebody once said: "Don't hang up. Just hold the line, and you'll get through in no time!"

36

A *Fill in the blanks with the word choices given. Change the word form if necessary.*

> avoid / suggest / communicate / thought / hang up

1. Doris _____ on her boyfriend after he kept arguing with her.

2. It's difficult to _____ getting wet when it's raining so hard.

3. Roy had a few _____ about the project.

4. The dark clouds in the sky _____ that we'll get rain this afternoon.

5. I don't have a phone, but we can _____ through e-mail.

B *Check the correct answers.*

1. What is the main idea of the article?
   - [ ] **a.** To explain how difficult it can be to speak in English
   - [ ] **b.** To show how important it is to use a phone when speaking English
   - [ ] **c.** To talk about how we can learn telephone English

2. Why is it good to see the person who is speaking English?
   - [ ] **a.** We can see things that can help us understand what they're saying.
   - [ ] **b.** We can stand closer to the person and hear better what they're saying.
   - [ ] **c.** We can tell him or her that we don't understand what has been said.

3. If we want a better idea of how a person feels, what should we look at when they speak?
   - [ ] **a.** His or her hands
   - [ ] **b.** His or her eyes
   - [ ] **c.** His or her lips

4. How can students of a foreign language feel when speaking it over the telephone?
   - [ ] **a.** Scared
   - [ ] **b.** Excited
   - [ ] **c.** Surprised

5. Why are phone conversations good for students of a foreign language?
   - [ ] **a.** Because people like to make phone calls.
   - [ ] **b.** Because students can seek them out very easily.
   - [ ] **c.** Because they can help improve their language skills.

37

Look at the two following conversations and take messages for the speakers.

Jack: Hey, Cindy. This is Jack. I need to talk to you about the …

Cindy: I'm not available at the moment. Leave your name and number after the beep, and I'll return your call. Have a great day!

Jack: Cindy. This is Jack Teller. I need to talk to you about Friday's high school reunion. I've got some bad news. The reunion has been postponed until next month. Call me when you get a chance. I hope to hear from you soon.

WHILE YOU WERE OUT

To: _____

From: _____

Message:

_____

_____

_____

_____

_____

_____

Sue: Hi, is May there?

Jane: She is out right now.

Sue: Do you know when she'll be back?

Jane: Sorry, I have no idea.

Sue: May I leave a message?

Jane: Sure.

Sue: Please tell her that I won't be in class tomorrow and to save the handouts for me. Also, please tell Mike that I can't meet him for lunch during the break.

Jane: OK.

Sue: Thanks! Goodbye!

Jane: Bye!

WHILE YOU WERE OUT

To: _____

From: _____

Message:

_____

_____

_____

_____

_____

_____

CHALLENGE YOURSELF

Part I Question & Response 🎧 1-15

Listen to the statement or question and choose the best response.

1. ☐ a   ☐ b   ☐ c   4. ☐ a   ☐ b   ☐ c
2. ☐ a   ☐ b   ☐ c   5. ☐ a   ☐ b   ☐ c
3. ☐ a   ☐ b   ☐ c

Part II Conversations 🎧 1-16

Listen to the conversation and answer the questions.

6. What does the woman say the man should do?
   ☐ a. Give James a better job
   ☐ b. Tell James to come upstairs
   ☐ c. Talk to James on the telephone
   ☐ d. Work with James

7. What can we say about Linda?
   ☐ a. She doesn't like being touched.
   ☐ b. She isn't answering her phone.
   ☐ c. She tried calling the girl.
   ☐ d. She's looking for something.

8. What is the woman asking the man?
   ☐ a. She wants to know if he is hanging up.
   ☐ b. She wants to know what's up.
   ☐ c. She wants to know the time.
   ☐ d. She wants to know his hobby.

9. What is the man asking about?
   ☐ a. What is on the chair
   ☐ b. What is happening
   ☐ c. Where he can sit
   ☐ d. When he should sit down

10. What do we know about the ring?
    ☐ a. The woman spent a lot of money on it.
    ☐ b. It is a gift for a woman.
    ☐ c. The man can only use it for a short time.
    ☐ d. There are no other rings the same as this one.

Linguaporta Training

Let's review the unit with Linguaporta.

39

WARM UP

TALK ABOUT THIS

Talk about these questions.

What chores do you do at home? Which chores do you dislike most? Why?

GEAR UP

A *Listen to the short talks and choose the correct pictures.* 1-17

Question 1.

Question 2.

UNIT
04

HOUSEHOLD CHORES

If you lived with roommates, how would you share the chores?

B *Role-play with a partner. Extend the conversation as much as you can.*

Ⓐ Can you do the laundry / do the dishes / take out the garbage for me?

Ⓑ OK. / No, it's your turn.
....

Ⓐ Did you clean your bedroom / the bathroom / the kitchen / the living room?

Ⓑ Yes, I did. / Not yet.
....

Ⓐ Would you mind cleaning the table / mopping the floor?

Ⓑ No problem. / I'm busy now.

41

Trading Places

A *Watch the video clip and check the correct answers.* WEB動画

1. Whose turn is it to do the washing this time?
   - ☐ **a.** Daniel's sister
   - ☐ **b.** Daniel's mom
   - ☐ **c.** Daniel himself

2. What is Daniel's excuse for not doing the chores?
   - ☐ **a.** It's not his turn to do the chores.
   - ☐ **b.** He wants to go out to play baseball.
   - ☐ **c.** He has an important date to go on.

3. What color were Barbie's pink T-shirts before?
   - ☐ **a.** White
   - ☐ **b.** Red
   - ☐ **c.** Pink

4. What's Daniel and Barbie's deal?
   - ☐ **a.** She does the wash this week, and he does it next week.
   - ☐ **b.** He covers for her when she has a secret date with Roger.
   - ☐ **c.** He helps wash her skirt this time only.

B *Listen to the conversation and fill in the blanks.* 🎧 1-18 🖥️

Daniel: Hey, sis. Can you do the wash for me? I want to go out with the guys and play baseball.

Barbie: Are you kidding? It's your ¹_____, and I'm not doing anything until it's my turn next Sunday.

Daniel: Oh, come on. I helped you out last time when you had a secret ²_____ with Roger, and you needed someone to cover for you.

Barbie: Yeah, and I'm still wearing pink T-shirts from when you forgot that there was a red sock in the whites and everything came out looking pink. You also shrunk my skirt from a large to a small when you washed it in the washing machine.

Daniel: Well, how was I ³_____ to know not to wash that?

Barbie: You could have read the ⁴_____ carefully. You know, the part about "Dry clean only"? That would have ⁵_____! Now I can't wear it without looking fat.

Daniel: You look fat anyway, and pink is a good color on you. It ⁶_____ your face.

Barbie: OK, that's it! I'm never doing the chores for you ever, ever again! You can forget your ball game.

Daniel: Fine! I'm telling Mom and Dad about your secret date with Roger!

Barbie: Well ... Maybe I could find the time to do your chores this week if you do them for me next week.

Daniel: OK, ⁷_____. See you later.

Barbie: I ⁸_____ you.

Daniel: You know I love you, my beautiful sister.

C *Practice the conversation with your partner.*

DISCUSSION

D *Discuss the following with your classmates.*

1. Did you have to do chores at your house as a kid?
2. How often do you do the laundry?
3. Did you ever trade chores with your siblings?

Active Voice VS. Passive Voice

> **S. + be + p.p. + (by somebody)**

Active They built the building.
        S.   V.   O.

Passive The building was built by them.
                      be + p.p.

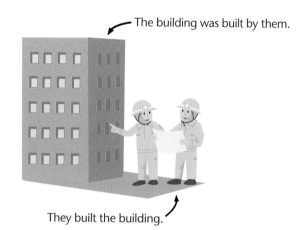

The building was built by them.

They built the building.

When to Use

Passive voice is used when the focus is on the action. It's not important to know who or what does the action.

- My money <u>was stolen</u>.
  we don't know who did the action

- The classrooms <u>are cleaned</u> every day by students.
  students are not important here, and the word can be removed

- The pyramid <u>was built</u> 5,000 years ago by ancient Egyptians.
  *we want to emphasize **pyramids** more than **ancient Egyptians***

Passive Voice Tenses

Tense	Sentence Pattern	Example
Present Simple	am/is/are + p.p.	The clothes are washed every day.
Past Simple	was/were + p.p.	My puppy was born last week.
Future Simple	will be + p.p. am/is/are going to be+ p.p.	The letters will be sent / are going to be sent soon.
Present Continuous	am/is/are + being + p.p.	The show is being watched by many people.
Present Perfect	have/has + been + p.p.	The killer has been arrested by the police.
Modals	can/may/should/have to/ has to ... + be + p.p.	This assignment should be finished before this Friday.

Work It Out

A *Change all the following **active voice** sentences into **passive voice** sentences.*

① The chef bakes the cakes every morning.
The cakes (☐ are baked / ☐ were baked) by the chef every morning.

② Uncle Tim changed the light bulb.
The light bulb (☐ is changed / ☐ was changed) by Uncle Tim.

③ A. A. Milne wrote *Winnie-the-Pooh* in 1926.
Winnie-the-Pooh (☐ was write / ☐ was written) by A. A. Milne in 1926.

④ We are doing the housework.
The housework (☐ is being done / ☐ is done) by us.

⑤ The teacher has corrected all the test papers.
All the test papers (☐ has been corrected / ☐ have been corrected) by the teacher.

B *Rewrite the following sentences using the passive voice.*

① Cindy has done the dishes.

_____

② Mike will not repair the bike.

_____

③ Sean has to finish the work before next Thursday.

_____

④ The police found the stolen car last Friday.

_____

⑤ The school is going to organize an outing.

_____

⑥ Beethoven composed the music.

_____

⑦ The typhoon caused great damage.

_____

⑧ A famous author will give a speech after dinner.

_____

Gender and Household Chores

🎧 1-19

Deciding who does the <u>chores</u> is one of the many challenges of marriage. Experts say that couples fight over chores almost as much as money. Husbands and wives often have different views about chores. But that doesn't mean there's no solution to their problems.

5　　Researchers say that men do less housework than women. Husbands also create more housework than their wives. One study asked married couples about household chores, and 74 percent of men said the chores were shared. Just 51 percent of women agreed.

Husbands and wives obviously have disagreements about chores. However, 10　it's possible to avoid fighting over household chores. Chores should be shared responsibilities. Experts say it's OK for husbands to do different chores than their wives. However, it's important to make sure that both the husband and wife work equally hard. Another piece of advice is to be flexible. Sometimes one might have to do the other person's chores.

15　　Couples should think of running the house as a business. The business will run well when grocery shopping, cleaning, cooking, and child-care are taken care of. However, if all the clothes are dirty, or there's no more milk in the refrigerator, or a child needs a ride to baseball practice and the car is out of gas, couples will argue. The key is to set goals and respect each other.

Ⓐ *Fill in the blanks with the word choices given. Change the word form if necessary.*

create / respect / housework / challenge / solution

1. Linda does most of her _____ on weekends.

2. For Clarence, Japanese class is a real _____.

3. Writers have to _____ characters for their books.

4. This writer is highly _____, and I like his books a lot.

5. The student found a perfect _____ to the problem and told the teacher.

Ⓑ *Check the correct answers.*

1. The underlined word "chores" means "small jobs that you _____."
   - ☐ **a.** wish to do every day
   - ☐ **b.** don't have to do very often
   - ☐ **c.** have to do regularly

2. What does the article say about husbands and wives?
   - ☐ **a.** Husbands and wives think differently about chores.
   - ☐ **b.** Every couple will fight over money and chores.
   - ☐ **c.** Husbands work a lot harder than their wives at home.

3. According to one study, what is NOT true about husbands?
   - ☐ **a.** Husbands generally create more housework than wives.
   - ☐ **b.** Husbands generally do more housework than wives.
   - ☐ **c.** Husbands generally do less housework than wives.

4. Which piece of advice is NOT mentioned in the article?
   - ☐ **a.** Be flexible with your partner about doing household chores.
   - ☐ **b.** Share the household chores with your partner equally.
   - ☐ **c.** Help your partner by doing extra household chores.

Ⓒ *How would you divide the household chores equally with your partner?*

You	Your Partner
1. Grocery shopping	

Look at the pictures and read the prompts. Then, write a passage around 150 words.

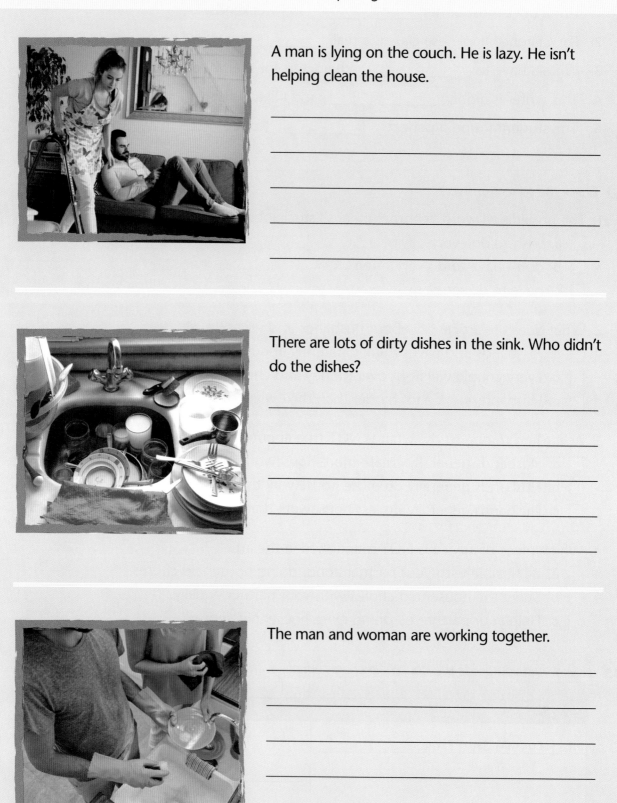

A man is lying on the couch. He is lazy. He isn't helping clean the house.

_____

_____

_____

_____

_____

There are lots of dirty dishes in the sink. Who didn't do the dishes?

_____

_____

_____

_____

_____

The man and woman are working together.

_____

_____

_____

_____

_____

CHALLENGE YOURSELF

Part I Question & Response 🎧 1-20

Listen to the statement or question and choose the best response.

1. ☐ a ☐ b ☐ c
2. ☐ a ☐ b ☐ c
3. ☐ a ☐ b ☐ c

4. ☐ a ☐ b ☐ c
5. ☐ a ☐ b ☐ c

Part II Conversations 🎧 1-21

Listen to the conversation and answer the questions.

6. What does the man say about himself?
   ☐ a. His body is really stiff and sore.
   ☐ b. He gets upset when he can't control things.
   ☐ c. He really likes sales.
   ☐ d. He is open to changes.

7. What happened to the woman's sweater?
   ☐ a. It was put in the garbage by mistake.
   ☐ b. It became smaller.
   ☐ c. It lost a lot of its color.
   ☐ d. It stretched and became bigger.

8. What is the man asking the woman?
   ☐ a. If she has a way to fix the problem
   ☐ b. If she was the one who caused the problem
   ☐ c. If she has ever had a problem like this before
   ☐ d. If she wants his help with the problem

9. What is the woman saying is important?
   ☐ a. To spend a lot of money on flowers
   ☐ b. To be polite and considerate
   ☐ c. To arrive early and stay late
   ☐ d. To stay home

10. Why hasn't the man cleaned up the mess in the kitchen?
   ☐ a. He says that it isn't his job.
   ☐ b. He says that it isn't his kitchen.
   ☐ c. He says that he didn't feel like it.
   ☐ d. He says that he wasn't home.

Linguaporta Training

Let's review the unit with Linguaporta.

Environmental Protection

WARM UP

TALK ABOUT THIS

Talk about these questions.

> Why is it important to protect our environment?

GEAR UP

A *Listen and look at the pictures below. What do you think is happening in each picture?* 🎧 1-22

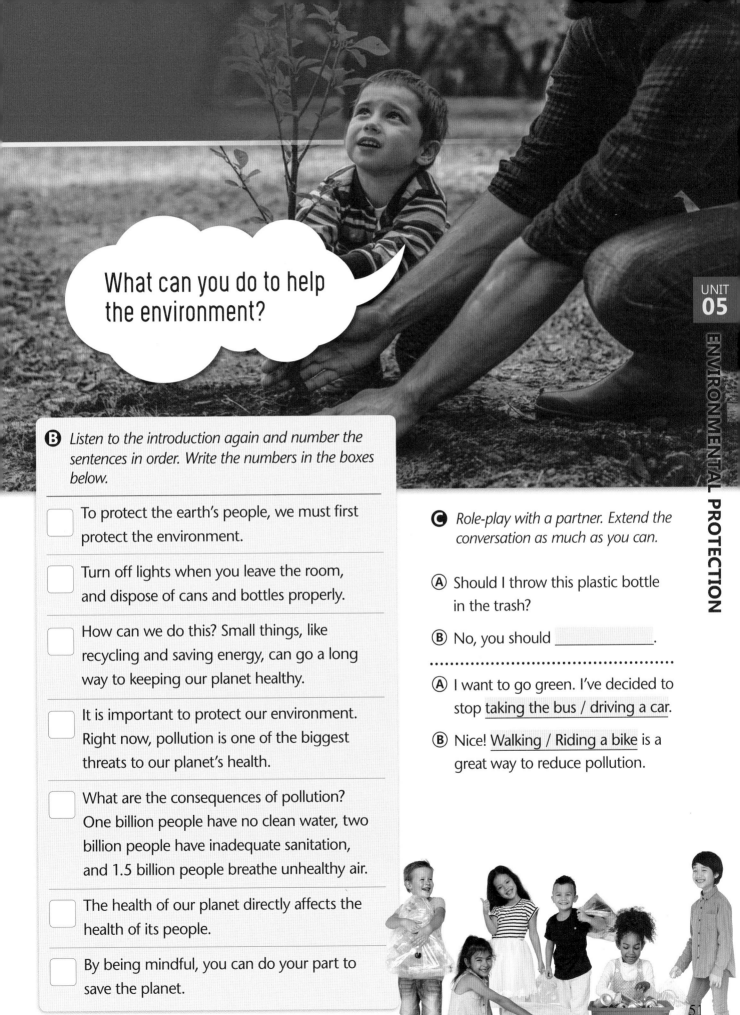

What can you do to help the environment?

B *Listen to the introduction again and number the sentences in order. Write the numbers in the boxes below.*

☐ To protect the earth's people, we must first protect the environment.

☐ Turn off lights when you leave the room, and dispose of cans and bottles properly.

☐ How can we do this? Small things, like recycling and saving energy, can go a long way to keeping our planet healthy.

☐ It is important to protect our environment. Right now, pollution is one of the biggest threats to our planet's health.

☐ What are the consequences of pollution? One billion people have no clean water, two billion people have inadequate sanitation, and 1.5 billion people breathe unhealthy air.

☐ The health of our planet directly affects the health of its people.

☐ By being mindful, you can do your part to save the planet.

C *Role-play with a partner. Extend the conversation as much as you can.*

Ⓐ Should I throw this plastic bottle in the trash?

Ⓑ No, you should _____.

. . . .

Ⓐ I want to go green. I've decided to stop taking the bus / driving a car.

Ⓑ Nice! Walking / Riding a bike is a great way to reduce pollution.

CLEAN UP YOUR ACT BY RECYCLING

A *Watch the video clip and check the correct answers.* WEB動画 💻

1. What kind of plates are the people using?
- ☐ **a.** Paper plates
- ☐ **b.** Recycled plates
- ☐ **c.** Plastic plates

2. Why does Andrea say we should treat our planet right?
- ☐ **a.** Because we only have one planet
- ☐ **b.** Because the government won't help
- ☐ **c.** Because not enough people are eco-friendly

3. What does Craig wish the government would do?
- ☐ **a.** Stop telling people what to do
- ☐ **b.** Stop the waste of natural resources
- ☐ **c.** Ask people to use only paper plates and cups

4. What will they do next?
- ☐ **a.** Start their own private landfill
- ☐ **b.** Throw the plastic cups and plates away
- ☐ **c.** Set up a recycling plan

B *Listen to the conversation and fill in the blanks.* 🎧 1-23 🖥️ WEB動画

Andrea, Craig, and Sam are finishing a meal.

Andrea: What a meal, Craig! But ... can you tell me why we're using paper cups and
¹_____? And what's with these plastic utensils?

Craig: After finishing our healthy meal, we can throw it all away. There ²_____ be
any hassles.

Sam: Great. We can start our own private ³_____.

Craig: Sam, would you stop all that doom and gloom and let me enjoy my meal?

Sam: Enjoy it ⁴_____ you can. The world's being destroyed. Pollution is causing
global warming, and global warming is causing floods and droughts.

Andrea: Sam's right. You really ⁵_____ to try to be more eco-friendly.

Craig: Could you explain what you mean?

Andrea: You treat your body right because you only have one. Well, we only have one
⁶_____. We should treat it right, too.

Craig: I know. I wish the government would stop people from wasting our natural
⁷_____. It's terrible!

Andrea: Why wait for the government to do something? Why don't you do something? You
have to think globally, but act ⁸_____.

Craig: You mean, think about world environmental problems, and do things in my own
town to make things better?

Andrea: Now you've got the idea!

C *Practice the conversation in a group.*

DISCUSSION

D *Discuss the following with your classmates.*

1. How has our environment changed over the past 30 years?

2. How does a higher global temperature affect our environment?

3. What will happen if ocean levels continue to rise?

UNIT
05

ENVIRONMENTAL PROTECTION

An indirect question is a question embedded inside a statement or another question. Indirect questions can end with a period rather than a question mark.

Direct Question
What time is it?

Indirect Question
I was wondering what time it is.

Indirect Questions with Yes/No Questions

*We use **if** or **whether** to introduce a yes-no question.*

> **Introductory Phrase** + **if/whether** + **S.** + **V.**

Direct Question	Indirect Question
Do you like playing basketball?	Could you tell me **if you like playing basketball?**
Are you living in London?	I'd like to know **if you are living in London.**
Did Nancy go shopping?	I'm not sure **whether** Nancy went shopping.
Was he an actor?	I wonder **whether** he was an actor.

Indirect Questions with Wh- Words

Direct Question	Indirect Question
What is she doing?	Do you know **what** she is doing?
Where are you from?	Could you tell me **where** you are from?
When is your birthday?	Can I ask **when** your birthday is?

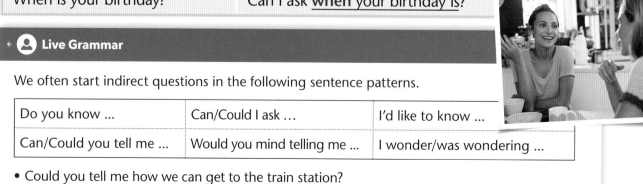

← 👤 Live Grammar

We often start indirect questions in the following sentence patterns.

Do you know …	Can/Could I ask …	I'd like to know …
Can/Could you tell me …	Would you mind telling me …	I wonder/was wondering …

• Could you tell me how we can get to the train station?

54   ➕ 🖼 📷 ♥   (Aa   ☺)

Work It Out

Ⓐ *Fill in the blanks with the words in the box.*

if / what / how often / when / where

① Do you mind _____ I open the window?

② Excuse me. Can you tell me _____ the restroom is?

③ I'd like to know _____ the movie starts.

④ Can I ask _____ time it is?

⑤ I wonder _____ you go to church.

Ⓑ *Change the **direct questions** into **indirect questions**.*

① Why are you crying?

He wants to know <u>why you are crying.</u> _____

② Where is your room?

She doesn't know _____

③ How old are you?

Can I ask _____

④ Can you swim?

I was wondering _____

⑤ Are you a student?

She's not sure _____

⑥ Who is your science teacher?

Would you mind telling me _____

⑦ Do you drink coffee every day?

Can you tell me _____

⑧ Is she single?

Tell me _____

ENVIRONMENTAL PROTECTION

One Small Step Toward a Cleaner Planet

🎧 1-24

On a hot day, nothing is quite as refreshing as a big cup of ice-cold tea from the local shop. But what happens to the cup once you're finished with your drink? If it's made of paper, it can easily be recycled; however, the same can't be said about the straw. The plastic used to make drinking straws is difficult to
5 recycle and takes a long time to break down. This is especially alarming because of the amount of plastic straws produced: Americans alone go through a shocking five hundred million straws per day.

Though drinking straws may be small, they make up a big portion of global plastic waste. Almost 90 percent of ocean trash is plastic, and plastic drinking
10 straws rank in the top 10 among all items collected during beach cleanups each year. Ninety percent of birds and many marine mammals—whales, dolphins, and seals—are said to have plastic in their systems.

What can be done to get rid of plastic drinking straws? The most obvious answer is to simply stop using straws altogether. While they may be convenient,
15 they certainly aren't a necessity. However, if you can't imagine life without drinking straws, there are alternatives to plastic ones. Glass straws, which come in a variety of colors and designs, tend to be very <u>durable</u>. Stainless steel straws can be cleaned in a dishwasher and often come with a bend that resembles that of common plastic straws. Bamboo straws, being made of a natural material, are
20 both disposable and biodegradable.

Getting rid of plastic straws might be a big and difficult pursuit, but it is an important step in making the world a better place.

A *Fill in the blanks with the word choices given. Change the word form if necessary.*

> obvious / material / especially / alarming / pursuit

1. The _____ of the box is very strong, so your bowl will be safe.
2. Jenny moved to the U.S. in _____ of a movie career.
3. The rainforest is disappearing at a(n) _____ rate.
4. You should wear comfortable shoes, _____ if you plan on walking far today.
5. One _____ example of a popular cartoon character is Mickey Mouse.

B *Check the correct answers.*

1. How many straws do Americans use per day?
   - ☐ **a.** One billion
   - ☐ **b.** Three hundred million
   - ☐ **c.** Five hundred million

2. What percentage of ocean trash is plastic?
   - ☐ **a.** Nearly 90 percent
   - ☐ **b.** Over 90 percent
   - ☐ **c.** About 50 percent

3. The underlined word "durable" means "staying in good condition _____."
   - ☐ **a.** only for a short time
   - ☐ **b.** for a long time
   - ☐ **c.** forever

4. Which of the following is NOT given as an alternative to plastic straws?
   - ☐ **a.** Paper straws
   - ☐ **b.** Glass straws
   - ☐ **c.** Bamboo straws

5. What do we know about stainless steel straws?
   - ☐ **a.** They don't have a bend.
   - ☐ **b.** They are disposable.
   - ☐ **c.** They can be cleaned in a dishwasher.

C *What steps would you take to help the environment?*

- _____
- _____
- _____

- _____
- _____
- _____

Look at the pictures and read the prompts. Then, write a passage around 150 words.

Beach Problems

Pollution is a big problem on our beaches.

_____

_____

_____

_____

_____

Trash is terrible for the ocean. How does trash affect sea creatures?

_____

_____

_____

_____

_____

There are ways we can help keep our beaches and oceans healthy.

_____

_____

_____

_____

_____

CHALLENGE YOURSELF

Part I Question & Response 🎧 1-25

Listen to the statement or question and choose the best response.

1. ☐ a ☐ b ☐ c
2. ☐ a ☐ b ☐ c
3. ☐ a ☐ b ☐ c

4. ☐ a ☐ b ☐ c
5. ☐ a ☐ b ☐ c

Part II Conversations 🎧 1-26

Listen to the conversation and answer the questions.

6. What does the woman say about pollution?
   - ☐ a. It is the fault of the U.S.
   - ☐ b. It is a problem of governments.
   - ☐ c. It is the worst problem we face.
   - ☐ d. It is a problem of the entire world.

7. What did the man say?
   - ☐ a. The woman should buy new baskets.
   - ☐ b. He will buy the woman new baskets.
   - ☐ c. The woman should use the baskets again.
   - ☐ d. The woman should throw away the baskets.

8. What might be true about the man and woman?
   - ☐ a. They're repairing their AC unit.
   - ☐ b. They're drinking a cool drink.
   - ☐ c. They're currently feeling very hot.
   - ☐ d. They're going to continue working.

9. What is true about the man and woman?
   - ☐ a. They're looking for jobs.
   - ☐ b. They're from New York.
   - ☐ c. They live in Florida.
   - ☐ d. They're moving with Tommy.

10. What might the woman help the man do?
   - ☐ a. Rinse out some glass bottles
   - ☐ b. Clean out the trash bin
   - ☐ c. Throw away the glass bottles
   - ☐ d. Put the clean dishes away

Linguaporta Training

Let's review the unit with Linguaporta.

UNIT
05

ENVIRONMENTAL PROTECTION

Bargaining for Fun

WARM UP

TALK ABOUT THIS

Talk about these questions.

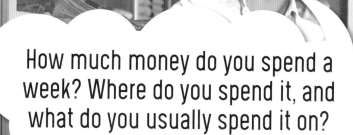

How much money do you spend a week? Where do you spend it, and what do you usually spend it on?

GEAR UP

Ⓐ *Listen to the conversations and choose the correct answer.* 1-27

Question 1.

What do the man and woman agree on?
- ☐ **a.** She shouldn't wear black.
- ☐ **b.** The man should wear light brown.
- ☐ **c.** She should wear a skirt, not a suit.

Question 2.

What does she say about her clothes?
- ☐ **a.** She says she needs a lot more brown clothes.
- ☐ **b.** She says that she's never bought beige clothes before.
- ☐ **c.** She suggests that she has too many brown clothes.

Question 3.

Why doesn't the woman want to buy the shoes?
- ☐ **a.** The pair of shoes is not suitable for her.
- ☐ **b.** She doesn't want to spend that much.
- ☐ **c.** This pair of shoes is of poor quality.

Question 4.

What does the man suggest the woman do?
- ☐ **a.** He thinks the woman should try them for a while.
- ☐ **b.** He believes that the gift is perfect for a friend.
- ☐ **c.** He suggests other items for her to look at.

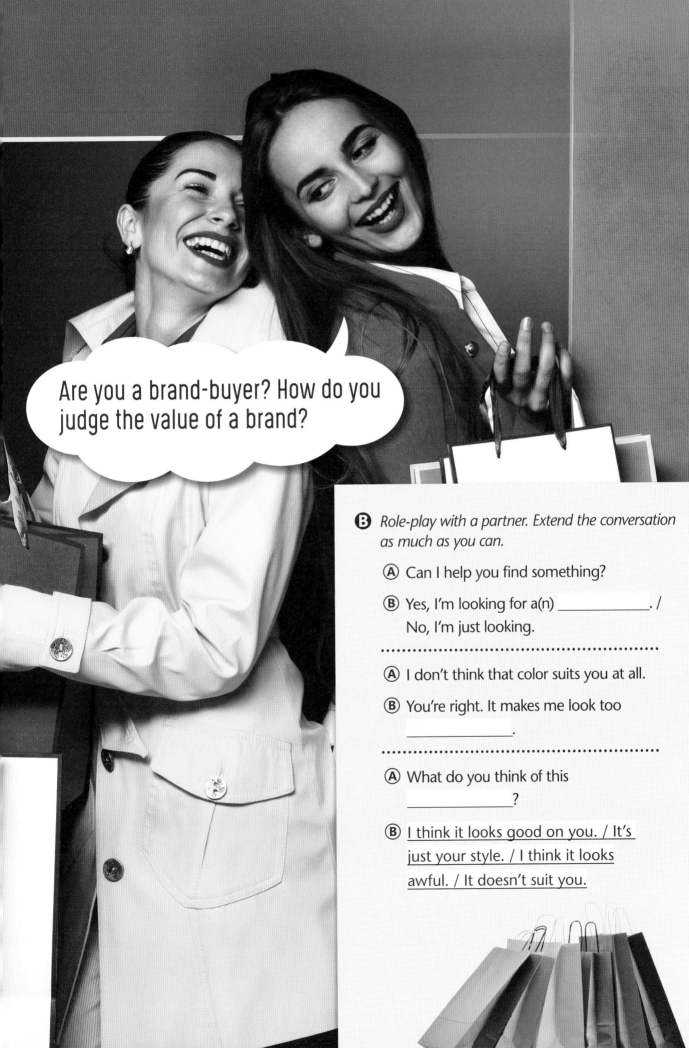

Are you a brand-buyer? How do you judge the value of a brand?

B *Role-play with a partner. Extend the conversation as much as you can.*

Ⓐ Can I help you find something?

Ⓑ Yes, I'm looking for a(n) _____. / No, I'm just looking.

....

Ⓐ I don't think that color suits you at all.

Ⓑ You're right. It makes me look too _____.

....

Ⓐ What do you think of this _____?

Ⓑ I think it looks good on you. / It's just your style. / I think it looks awful. / It doesn't suit you.

Snappy Shopper

A *Watch the video clip and check the correct answers.* WEB動画

1. What has Karen been looking for?
- ☐ **a.** A dress
- ☐ **b.** A handbag
- ☐ **c.** Silver spangles

2. What does Karen do?
- ☐ **a.** She's a street vendor.
- ☐ **b.** She's a student.
- ☐ **c.** She's a teacher.

3. How much does the street vendor offer Karen first?
- ☐ **a.** 20 dollars
- ☐ **b.** 15 dollars
- ☐ **c.** 13 dollars

4. In the end, how much discount does Karen get?
- ☐ **a.** 20 percent
- ☐ **b.** 30 percent
- ☐ **c.** 50 percent

B *Listen to the conversation and fill in the blanks.* 🎧 1-28 💻

Karen is wandering along the street with her friend Sarah.

Karen: Sarah, look! I found something I've been looking for for weeks.

Sarah: What is it?

Karen: My [1]_____ handbag. It looks elegant and, it goes well with my dress.

Sarah: Come on, you have many bags to go with your dress!

Karen: Sarah!

While Sarah is complaining, Karen talks to a street vendor.

Karen: How much is the handbag?

Vendor: You mean the one with silver spangles and [2]_____?

Karen: Yes.

Vendor: That one is $20. Since you like it so much, I'll give you a good [3]_____.
Are you a student?

Karen: Yes, yes, yes! How much will you [4]_____ a poor student?

Vendor: Well, $15 is my final [5]_____.

Karen: No, no, no ... Can you give it to me a little bit cheaper?

Vendor: $13, no more [6]_____. It's already very cheap!

Karen: I only have $10.

Vendor: OK, $10. Here you go.

Sarah: Karen, you do [7]_____ me a lot.

Karen: Call me the shopping [8]_____!

C *Practice the conversation in a group.*

DISCUSSION

D *Discuss the following with your classmates.*

1. Have you ever bargained for an item?
2. Do you like to buy clothing from street vendors?
3. Why do some people say we must bargain in
   certain countries?

An adverbial clause begins with a subordinate conjunction such as when, while, before, until, because, so that, etc.

- John walked the dog while Jane was mopping.

To Express Time

as / while

*We use **as** and **while** to express two things happening at the same time. The adverbial clause is usually in a **continuous tense**.*

- Mary did the dishes **while** Tom was sleeping.

- **As** Cindy was walking down the stairs, everyone turned to watch.

when

*We use **when** to emphasize the time something happens. The adverbial clause is usually in a **simple** or **continuous tense**.*

- I lost my ring **when/while** I was doing the dishes.

- **When** her name was called, she raised her hand.

since

> **present perfect**, **since** + **simple past**

- I have been busy working **since** I graduated from college.

before / after

***Before** and **after** can be both conjunctions and prepositions. **Gerunds (V-ing)** are put after them as prepositions.*

- **Before** Howard entered the house, he took off his shoes.

- **After** you finish your story, I want to tell you something.

- Nina feels much better **after** taking medicine.

until / not ... until

***until:** to express a continuous action*
***not ... until:** to express an action finished in a short time*

- I stayed at the office **until** I finished my work.
  - = I did **not** leave the office **until** I finished my work.

To Express Reason

because / because of

> because + S. + V.
> because of + N.

- I don't want to go shopping because I don't have money.
- Because of the rain, the game had to be canceled.

as / since

As and *since* are usually put at the beginning of the sentence.

- As you've already heard the news, I won't repeat it.
- Since no one can figure out the answer, let's ask the teacher for help.

To Express Purpose

so that

Sometimes we can use so *instead of* so that. So *can be used to express both the* result *and* purpose.

- Pam is getting another job so that she can travel abroad.
  = Pam is getting another job so as to / in order to travel abroad.
- I bought the book so (that) I could read it.
- I'm sick, so I didn't go to school today.

Work It Out

A *Fill in the blanks with the word choices given.*

so / when / since / because of / until

① Our departure was delayed _____ bad weather.
② Eddie didn't get up _____ his mother came back.
③ She has lost seven pounds _____ she started to exercise.
④ The thieves started running _____ they saw the police.
⑤ My knee started hurting, _____ I stopped running.

B *Combine the two sentences using the hints given.*

① We left early. / We would not miss our train. (so that)

_____

② No one wants to work with Willy. / People find him difficult to get along with. (because)

_____

③ You feel dizzy. / You should sit down and get some rest. (since)

_____

④ Most people work. / Most people make money for the things they need. (in order to)

_____

65

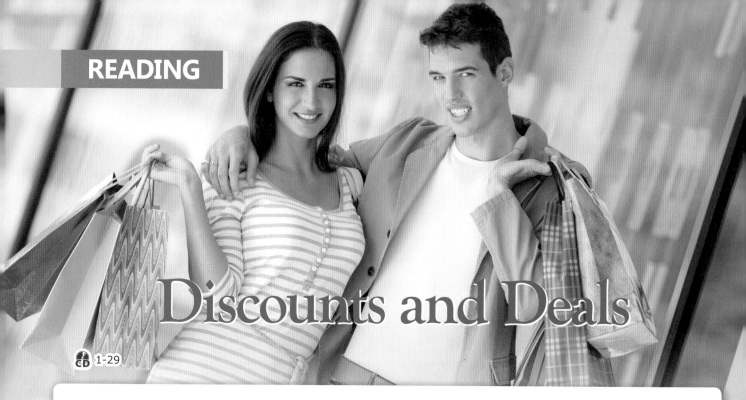

Discounts and Deals

🎵 1-29

For many of us, shopping is like a sport. Getting a great deal on a designer-label handbag or a trendy mobile phone can feel like hitting a home run. Sometimes, shopping can be a battle of wills between the buyer and seller. If you want to be a tough customer and drive a real hard bargain, then you need to master the art of
5 bargaining. Great deals can be found almost everywhere —the secret is in knowing how to ask and never giving up.

Of course, a night market is a bargainer's paradise. There you can bargain to your heart's content. But you need to be a good judge of quality, or the great bargain you thought you got can turn out to be the exact opposite: a <u>rip-off</u>.

10 Unlike night markets, department store prices are usually fixed, so bargaining is no picnic. However, if you notice a small flaw in an item, you shouldn't hesitate to ask for a discount. If the clerk refuses to lower the price, ask for a VIP card instead. Keep an eye on sales and special promotions, as these can be a shopper's best friends.

Always be a clever traveler. At the airport check-in desk, ask for an upgrade to first
15 or business class. Call hotels directly and ask for upgrades or low-season rates. Free breakfast, airport pickup, and other freebies are fair game as well.

The last word on shopping and bargaining: Keep asking, and you shall receive. Now go out there and hit a home run!

A *Fill in the blanks with the word choices given. Change the word form if necessary.*

> clever / battle / flaw / content / refuse

1. I returned the product because it had a _____ in it.

2. Martha asked Bob to leave, but he _____.

3. Jason is quite _____ and does well at school.

4. Andrew is going on a trip to a nearby lake so that he can fish to his heart's _____.

5. The _____ lasted three days, but there was peace after it ended.

B *Check the correct answers.*

1. What is the secret of getting a great deal?
   - [ ] **a.** Making friends with the seller
   - [ ] **b.** Just shopping in a night market
   - [ ] **c.** Knowing how to ask and never giving up

2. According to the writer, how do you bargain in a department store?
   - [ ] **a.** Try offering half the clerk's starting price or a little more.
   - [ ] **b.** You should shop with a major credit card or gift certificates.
   - [ ] **c.** If you see a small flaw in something, ask for a discount.

3. When should you ask for a VIP card?
   - [ ] **a.** When there is a great special promotion
   - [ ] **b.** When the clerk refuses to lower the price
   - [ ] **c.** When something is going to be a rip-off

4. Which of the following is NOT recommended in getting a good deal when traveling?
   - [ ] **a.** Asking for an upgrade to first or business class at the airport
   - [ ] **b.** Bargaining in a department store to your heart's content
   - [ ] **c.** Seeing if hotels provide a complimentary breakfast or airport pickup

5. The underlined word "rip-off" means a(n) _____ copy of something.
   - [ ] **a.** cheap
   - [ ] **b.** original
   - [ ] **c.** excellent

C *What are your tips for bargaining or being a clever customer? Share with your classmates.*

_____
_____
_____

Read the paragraph and the sample article. What would you do if you won the grand prize?

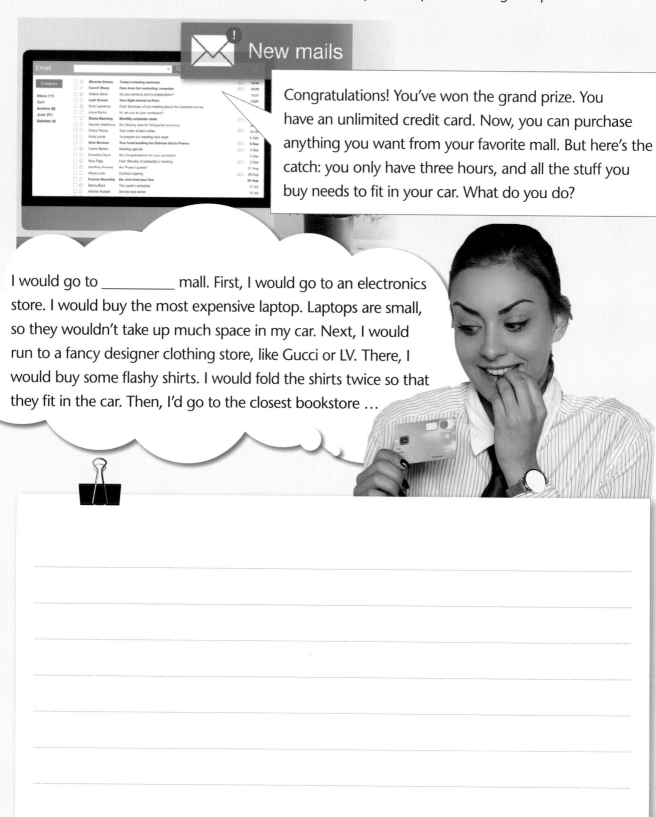

New mails

Congratulations! You've won the grand prize. You have an unlimited credit card. Now, you can purchase anything you want from your favorite mall. But here's the catch: you only have three hours, and all the stuff you buy needs to fit in your car. What do you do?

I would go to _____ mall. First, I would go to an electronics store. I would buy the most expensive laptop. Laptops are small, so they wouldn't take up much space in my car. Next, I would run to a fancy designer clothing store, like Gucci or LV. There, I would buy some flashy shirts. I would fold the shirts twice so that they fit in the car. Then, I'd go to the closest bookstore …

CHALLENGE YOURSELF

Part I **Question & Response** 🎧 1-30

Listen to the statement or question and choose the best response.

1. ☐ a   ☐ b   ☐ c   4. ☐ a   ☐ b   ☐ c
2. ☐ a   ☐ b   ☐ c   5. ☐ a   ☐ b   ☐ c
3. ☐ a   ☐ b   ☐ c

Part II **Conversations** 🎧 1-31

Listen to the conversation and answer the questions.

6. What does the woman say about Jane?
   ☐ a. She will have enough money.
   ☐ b. She is nice and will make friends easily.
   ☐ c. She is smart enough to take care of herself.
   ☐ d. She will ask for help if she needs to.

7. What does the man say about the dinner?
   ☐ a. He had as much as he wanted.
   ☐ b. He wanted to have more to eat.
   ☐ c. He was not very hungry.
   ☐ d. He thought it was OK.

8. What does the man NOT want to do?
   ☐ a. Deal with any big crowds of people
   ☐ b. Eat any foods he doesn't like
   ☐ c. Try to get cheaper prices when shopping
   ☐ d. Play any games he won't be able to win

9. What does the woman say she did today?
   ☐ a. She visited a friend.
   ☐ b. She went out for a walk.
   ☐ c. She exercised at the gym.
   ☐ d. She prepared their dinner.

10. What does the woman say about the man's watch?
   ☐ a. She thinks it is very expensive.
   ☐ b. She thinks it is strange-looking.
   ☐ c. She thinks he got a good deal on it.
   ☐ d. She thinks it looks very beautiful.

Linguaporta Training

Let's review the unit with Linguaporta.

UNIT
06

BARGAINING FOR FUN

69

Part I   1-32

Listen to the statement or question and check the best response.

1. ☐ a ☐ b ☐ c   3. ☐ a ☐ b ☐ c
2. ☐ a ☐ b ☐ c   4. ☐ a ☐ b ☐ c

Part II   1-33

Listen to the conversation and check the correct answer.

1. What did the woman do?
   - ☐ **a.** Took a picture of the forest
   - ☐ **b.** Took a picture of herself
   - ☐ **c.** Posted a message online
   - ☐ **d.** Chatted with her friends online

2. What are they using?
   - ☐ **a.** A modem
   - ☐ **b.** A printer
   - ☐ **c.** A scanner
   - ☐ **d.** A mouse

3. What did NOT George do?
   - ☐ **a.** Clean the dirty plates
   - ☐ **b.** Take out the trash
   - ☐ **c.** Clean the floor
   - ☐ **d.** Wash the clothes

4. What is James going to do?
   - ☐ **a.** Take an aspirin for his headache
   - ☐ **b.** Buy a more comfortable bed
   - ☐ **c.** Rub and massage his sore eyes
   - ☐ **d.** Change the time he goes to bed

Part III 1-34

Listen to the short passage and check the correct picture.

1.
 ☐ a
 ☐ b
 ☐ c

2.
 ☐ a
 ☐ b
 ☐ c

Part IV

Fill in the blanks.

> weight / housework / electrical / energy / label /
> essential / informed / communicate / hang up / uploaded

1. Don sells different kinds of _____ equipment.

2. The teacher _____ the class that there would be a test on Friday.

3. My doctor said I had to lose _____.

4. I slept great and have lots of _____ today!

5. We sometimes call each other, but we usually _____ by e-mail.

6. You can't use your phone here. _____, please.

7. Frank _____ a video of his dog to an online site.

8. Bonnie stayed home on Saturday to do _____.

9. There is a _____ on the package that shows the price of the item.

10. Flour is _____ for making bread.

Part V

Check the correct answer.

1. Telephone conversations can be daunting for anyone if spoken in a language that is still being _____.
   - ☐ **a.** learned
   - ☐ **b.** learning
   - ☐ **c.** to learn
   - ☐ **d.** learn

2. I've lived in this town _____ I was young.
   - ☐ **a.** never
   - ☐ **b.** since
   - ☐ **c.** during
   - ☐ **d.** when

3. This was the place _____ I first met my husband.
   - ☐ **a.** which
   - ☐ **b.** where
   - ☐ **c.** when
   - ☐ **d.** that

4. _____ alcohol could also lead to late night eating.
   - ☐ **a.** Drink
   - ☐ **b.** Drinking
   - ☐ **c.** Drank
   - ☐ **d.** Drinks

5. The war broke out in 1979, which is _____ I was born.
   - ☐ **a.** on which
   - ☐ **b.** where
   - ☐ **c.** for which
   - ☐ **d.** when

6. Don't be so hard _____ him! Look at those big puppy eyes!
   - ☐ **a.** on
   - ☐ **b.** over
   - ☐ **c.** about
   - ☐ **d.** to

7. Both mothers and fathers play important roles in _____ children.
   - ☐ **a.** arising
   - ☐ **b.** rising
   - ☐ **c.** raising
   - ☐ **d.** risking

8. _____ night markets, department store prices are usually fixed.
   - ☐ **a.** Dislike
   - ☐ **b.** Unlike
   - ☐ **c.** Likely
   - ☐ **d.** Likes

9. Could you tell me _____ from?
   - ☐ **a.** where you
   - ☐ **b.** where are
   - ☐ **c.** where you are
   - ☐ **d.** where are you

10. Pam is getting another job _____ she can travel abroad.
    - ☐ **a.** so that
    - ☐ **b.** so as to
    - ☐ **c.** in order to
    - ☐ **d.** in order

Read the article and check the correct answer.

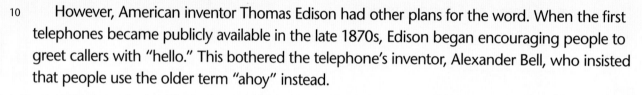

When you first began studying English, one of the earliest things you probably learned to say was "hello." This greeting is so common that you may assume the word "hello" has been used in this way since the
5 <u>dawn</u> of the English language.

However, it wasn't all that long ago that saying "hello" meant something entirely different. The first recorded use of "hello" occurred in 1827. At that time, it was used to get someone's attention, much like the phrase "excuse me."

10   However, American inventor Thomas Edison had other plans for the word. When the first telephones became publicly available in the late 1870s, Edison began encouraging people to greet callers with "hello." This bothered the telephone's inventor, Alexander Bell, who insisted that people use the older term "ahoy" instead.

In the end, it was the publishers of the first phone books that settled the debate. These
15 phone books came with instructions on how to use the newly invented telephone. In these instructions, "hello" was listed as the proper greeting to use. [   ], with the spread of the telephone, "hello" soon became the everyday greeting we know so well today.

1. Which is similar in meaning to the underlined word "dawn"?
  ☐ **a.** beginning
  ☐ **b.** prosperity
  ☐ **c.** spread

2. In 1827, the word "hello" was used to _____ someone.
  ☐ **a.** greet
  ☐ **b.** pay attention to
  ☐ **c.** attract attention of

3. Which sentence is true?
  ☐ **a.** Thomas Edison insisted that people use the term "ahoy."
  ☐ **b.** The first phone books listed "hello" as the proper greeting to use.
  ☐ **c.** The first telephones became publicly available in the first half of 19th century.

4. The word that belongs in the [   ] in this article is _____.
  ☐ **a.** Instead
  ☐ **b.** However
  ☐ **c.** Consequently

5. What is the best title for this passage?

☐ **a.** The First Recorded Use of "Hello"

☐ **b.** Why We Say "Hello"

☐ **c.** Difference Between "Hello" and "Ahoy"

Part VII

Look at the picture and write a paragraph of "Easy Ways to Get Exercise" in 80-120 words.

WARM UP

TALK ABOUT THIS

Talk about these questions.

> What rules do you have at home?

GEAR UP

A *Listen and look at the pictures below. What do you think is happening in each picture?* 🔊 2-01

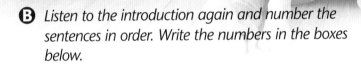

Describe your relationship with your parents. What do you like and dislike about it?

B *Listen to the introduction again and number the sentences in order. Write the numbers in the boxes below.*

☐ See what you can do about having family nights. You could go out for dinner, go bowling, sit around, and play cards all night with your family.

☐ "How can I have a better relationship with my parents?"

☐ On the other hand, children feel alienated and unfulfilled with their home life and relationships with parents as well. Do you have any helpful suggestions to improve a relationship?

☐ There is no one answer to the question, but first, maybe you can sit down with your parents and tell them that you want to improve your relationship with them and that you are willing to do everything in your power to make it work.

☐ Many families have relationship problems. Parents feel helpless and frustrated when their kids get into bad situations.

C *Role-play with a partner. Extend the conversation as much as you can.*

Ⓐ How's your family?

Ⓑ <u>Great! / Couldn't be better! / Not bad.</u>

···

Ⓐ How many brothers or sisters do you have?

Ⓑ I have _____.

···

Ⓐ How's your relationship with your family?

Ⓑ <u>Good. / Bad. / Frustrating.</u>

75

A Father's Lessons

A *Watch the video clip and check the correct answers.* WEB動画 🖥️

1. What is Anna's father's job at present?
- [ ] **a.** He is a police officer.
- [ ] **b.** He is a chef.
- [ ] **c.** He is a taxi driver.

2. Who helped Anna's father get a job as a chef?
- [ ] **a.** A taxi driver
- [ ] **b.** A businessman
- [ ] **c.** A firefighter

3. Why did Anna's father's business fail?
- [ ] **a.** Customers didn't like his product.
- [ ] **b.** He didn't manage money well.
- [ ] **c.** He failed a business exam.

4. What can we learn from Anna's father?
- [ ] **a.** Never give up
- [ ] **b.** Quit after you fail
- [ ] **c.** Go to business school

B *Listen to the conversation and fill in the blanks.* 🎧 2-02 💻 WEB動画

Anna: Dad, I'm going to be graduating from university soon. But I feel like I have no ¹_____ in life.

Dad: You know, when I was your age, I was ²_____, too.

Anna: Really? Tell me everything.

Dad: I wanted the freedom of owning my own business. So I followed my dream and opened a store. But I didn't manage my money well and, as a result, went ³_____.

Anna: Oh no! That's so sad.

Dad: It's OK. It was my ⁴_____. But I learned something from my failure. Having experience is extremely important.

Anna: I'll remember that. What did you do next?

Dad: I tried to become a police officer and then a firefighter, but I failed again. So I became a taxi driver.

Anna: What was that like?

Dad: It was nice. I met all kinds of people. One day, I ⁵_____ up a conversation with a businessman. He had just opened a restaurant. I told him I loved cooking. Then—amazingly—he offered me a job.

Anna: So that's how you became a ⁶_____. It was an accident! That passenger got you the job.

Dad: Yep. Looking back now, I can see that I had a lot of ⁷_____ experiences.

Anna: Even though you had so many failures?

Dad: Yes. Never a day goes by when I ⁸_____ my failures. They led me to where I am today.

Anna: Thanks for sharing your story. I think I know what I should do now.

Dad: I'm happy I could help you. I'm always here if you need me. That's a promise.

C *Practice the conversation with your partner.*

DISCUSSION

D *Discuss the following with your classmates.*

1. Do you think that your father is tougher than your mother?
2. Did your father teach you different things than your mother?
3. Do fathers push sons harder than daughters?

77

Causative verbs express the idea of someone causing something to take place.

My mother made me clean my room.

have

S. + **have** + O. + V.
S. + **have** + O. + p.p.

- My mother **had** Sarah **do** the dishes.
- Let's **have** our house **painted** this summer.

make

S. + **make** + O. + V.
S. + **make** + O. + p.p.

- No one can **make** me **do** it if I don't want to.
- The announcer **made** the information **known** to the public.

get

S. + **get** + O. + **to** + V.
S. + **get** + O. + p.p.

- Sally wants to **get** her kids **to eat** more vegetables.
- I **got** my hair **cut** yesterday, but I don't like how it looks.

let

S. + **let** + O. + V.
S. + **let** + O. + **be** + p.p.

- She would not **let** her child **do** the housework.
- The engineer **let** his analysis **be reviewed**.

help

S. + **help** + O. + (**to**) + V.

- Nancy **helps** her mother **take out** the garbage.

Work It Out

A *Fill in the blanks with the words provided.*

go / to clean / call / cut / ask / let

① The parents _____ the children _____ their room once a week.

② She wouldn't _____ her little brother _____ home by himself.

③ I'll have Greg _____ you back as soon as possible.

④ Jason doesn't get his hair _____ regularly.

B *Combine the two sentences using causative verbs.*

① Tina did her homework. / Tina's brother helped her do it.

_____

② Professor Brown's students read four novels in a week. / He made them do it.

_____

③ Dora doesn't have a dog. / Dora's parents wouldn't let her.

_____

GRAMMAR   ## 2 Inverted Sentences

Inverted sentences are used as a means of applying stress or emphasis. An inverted sentence switches the placement of the verb to before the subject of a sentence.

Negative Adverbs

never, seldom, little, hardly, not only ... but also, not ... until

- It has **never** been easy to learn English.
  We use statements to describe a general idea.

  Never is emphasized in this sentence.
= **Never** <u>has it been</u> easy to learn English.
  aux. + S. + V.

- She is seldom late for work.
  = **Seldom** <u>is she</u> late for work.
    be V. + S.

- We little believed that he would lie.
  = **Little** <u>did we believe</u> that he would lie.
    aux. + S. + V.

- I had hardly arrived home when my phone rang.
  = **Hardly** <u>had I arrived</u> home when my
    aux. + S. + V.
  phone rang.

- Tanya not only loves her daughter, but she (also) trusts her.
  = **Not only** <u>does Tanya love</u> her daughter,
    aux. + S. + V.
  she (also) trusts her.

- He didn't go home until he finished his work.
  = **Not until** he finished his work
    <u>did he go</u> home.
    aux. + S. + V.

Adverbs of Place

- A cat lies **under the table.**

  Under the table is emphasized in this sentence.

= **Under the table** <u>lies a cat.</u>
    V. + S.

- An old house stood on top of the hill.
  = **On top of the hill** <u>stood an old house.</u>
      V. + S.

- Here <u>comes the bus.</u> = Here <u>it comes.</u>
    V. + S.   *When the subject is a pronoun (it), it doesn't need to be inverted.*

Work It Out

Rewrite the sentences as inverted sentences based on the hints given.

① I haven't ever felt so excited. (never)

_____

② She doesn't eat beef very often. (seldom)

_____

③ I didn't dream of seeing her again. (little)

_____

FATHERS IN THE ANIMAL KINGDOM

🎵 2-03

   Both mothers and fathers play important roles in raising children. However, newborn babies need mothers much more than fathers. After all, a mother carries a baby for nine months, and once born, the baby needs a mother's milk to survive. This is something a father simply cannot provide.

5   But in the animal world, the familiar roles of mother and father are sometimes opposite to what we expect. For example, female seahorses deposit their eggs into the male's abdomen. The male seahorse then carries the babies, nourishing them until they are born. Can you imagine your father pregnant with your little brother or sister?

10   Male seahorses aren't unique. Emperor penguin dads, not moms, sit on eggs in the nest to keep them warm. In different species of frogs, fathers carry unhatched eggs on their backs and in their vocal pouches. These dads know what it's really like to have a frog in their throats!

   Our fathers help raise us, and the same is true for animal fathers and their 15 young. Those emperor penguin fathers work together with mothers to keep their chicks off the ice and feed them food from their own stomachs. And wolves also make good dads. Besides feeding and protecting their young, wolf dads like to play with them and teach them about survival.

   Indeed, fathers take care of their young in many ways, and the effort they 20 put in is essential. So don't forget to tell your dad how much you love him. Don't forget to tell your dad how much you appreciate what he does for you.

Ⓐ *Fill in the blanks with the word choices given. Change the word form if necessary.*

> essential / effort / pregnant / raise / role

1. Joe's parents died when he was a baby, and he was _____ by his grandparents.

2. My friends played an important _____ in my life when I was growing up.

3. Water and sunlight are _____ for plants to grow.

4. It didn't take Jessica much _____ to learn how to drive a car.

5. Margaret is _____ and expecting to give birth in June.

Ⓑ *Check the correct answers.*

1. Which of the following statements is correct?
   - ☐ **a.** Fathers play a more important role in raising children.
   - ☐ **b.** In the animal kingdom, the roles of father and mother are never reversed.
   - ☐ **c.** Animal fathers, like human fathers, help to raise their young.

2. What kind of animal father carries the baby until it is born?
   - ☐ **a.** The emperor penguin
   - ☐ **b.** The wolf
   - ☐ **c.** The seahorse

3. How are emperor penguin dads different from seahorses?
   - ☐ **a.** Emperor penguin dads sit on eggs.
   - ☐ **b.** Emperor penguin dads carry eggs in their abdomens.
   - ☐ **c.** Seahorses carry eggs in their throats.

4. Where do mother seahorses put their eggs?
   - ☐ **a.** In the male's mid-section
   - ☐ **b.** In a nest
   - ☐ **c.** In the male's vocal pouch

5. Which statement about animal parents is true?
   - ☐ **a.** Wolf dads don't like to play with their young.
   - ☐ **b.** Female seahorses carry their eggs in their abdomen.
   - ☐ **c.** Frog fathers keep unhatched eggs in their vocal pouches.

WRITING

Hi, everyone! It's the season for sharing, so invite your friends and family to celebrate! You don't always need a reason to get together with them. Invite them to share your happiness now! Look at the sample article and write your own invitations.

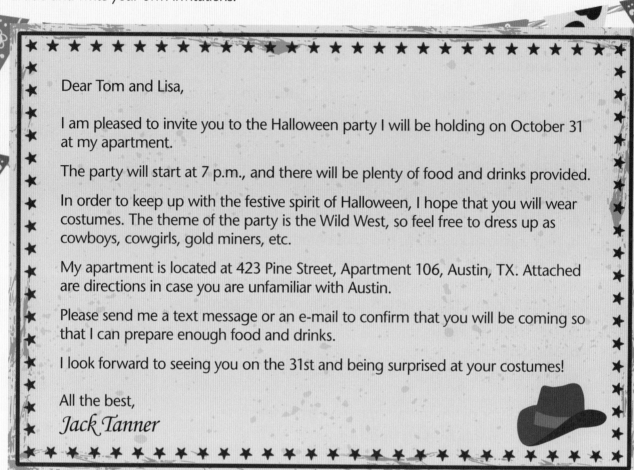

Dear Tom and Lisa,

I am pleased to invite you to the Halloween party I will be holding on October 31 at my apartment.

The party will start at 7 p.m., and there will be plenty of food and drinks provided.

In order to keep up with the festive spirit of Halloween, I hope that you will wear costumes. The theme of the party is the Wild West, so feel free to dress up as cowboys, cowgirls, gold miners, etc.

My apartment is located at 423 Pine Street, Apartment 106, Austin, TX. Attached are directions in case you are unfamiliar with Austin.

Please send me a text message or an e-mail to confirm that you will be coming so that I can prepare enough food and drinks.

I look forward to seeing you on the 31st and being surprised at your costumes!

All the best,
Jack Tanner

CHALLENGE YOURSELF

Part I Question & Response 🎧 2-04

Listen to the statement or question and choose the best response.

1. ☐ a   ☐ b   ☐ c
2. ☐ a   ☐ b   ☐ c
3. ☐ a   ☐ b   ☐ c

4. ☐ a   ☐ b   ☐ c
5. ☐ a   ☐ b   ☐ c

Part II Conversations 🎧 2-05

Listen to the conversation and answer the questions.

6. Why does the man want to move out?
   ☐ a. He wants to get married and have children.
   ☐ b. He is tired of being treated like a baby.
   ☐ c. His sister is always bothering him.
   ☐ d. His wife is going to have another baby.

7. What is the man saying?
   ☐ a. He is not yet used to his new job.
   ☐ b. The subway system is great in New York.
   ☐ c. He wants to find some furniture, first.
   ☐ d. He wants to be more familiar with the city.

8. What is mentioned about the dog?
   ☐ a. It is not a puppy anymore.
   ☐ b. It is very small and easy to carry.
   ☐ c. It can do a lot of tricks.
   ☐ d. It is sick and sleeps a lot.

9. What is the man saying?
   ☐ a. Winter sports are a lot of fun.
   ☐ b. Transportation is very expensive.
   ☐ c. Canadian winters are very uncomfortable.
   ☐ d. People in Canada have bad habits.

10. What does the man say about Mike?
    ☐ a. He doesn't get paid for his work.
    ☐ b. He finished his presentation quickly.
    ☐ c. He wasn't on time for his presentation.
    ☐ d. He spent a lot of time on the presentation.

Linguaporta Training

Let's review the unit with Linguaporta.

UNIT 08

Culture Shock

WARM UP

TALK ABOUT THIS

Talk about these questions.

> Have you ever experienced culture shock?

GEAR UP

A *Listen and look at the pictures below. What do you think is happening in each picture?*  2-06

Which factor would be your biggest culture shock: food, language, environment, or something else?

B *Listen to the introduction again and number the sentences in order. Write the numbers in the boxes below.*

☐ The use of language was different, the food was different, and the material we were studying in school was different.

☐ I moved to West Virginia when I was 13. After living in New Jersey, Hawaii, California, and Portugal, West Virginia was a culture shock to me.

☐ It's important to feel comfortable in a new place. Try not to force yourself to change too fast or to change too many things at once. Let yourself adjust to changes at your own pace.

☐ Appreciating the variety that a new culture offers can be interesting instead of frustrating.

☐ Try to stay open to new ways of doing things. Take time to notice the things that are the same and the things that are different.

☐ To understand culture shock, it helps us to understand what culture is. The different environment has a big effect on our attitudes and behavior as well.

C *Role-play with a partner. Extend the conversation as much as you can.*

Ⓐ How do you feel when you <u>travel / move</u> to a new place?

Ⓑ I feel <u>excited / challenged / sad / lonely</u>.

· ·

Ⓐ How long did it take you to get used to being here?

Ⓑ It took me <u>a while / several months</u>.

85

Don't Forget the Tip !

Ⓐ *Watch the video clip and check the correct answers.*

1. What did Jack almost forget to do?
   - ☐ **a.** Pay for his meal
   - ☐ **b.** Leave a tip after his meal
   - ☐ **c.** Take his leftovers

2. How much should you tip at restaurants in the United States?
   - ☐ **a.** Exactly 20 percent
   - ☐ **b.** Around 10 or 15 percent
   - ☐ **c.** Between 15 and 20 percent

3. Why was the taxi driver angry?
   - ☐ **a.** Jack only tipped him 5 percent.
   - ☐ **b.** Jack only gave him one dollar for carrying his bags.
   - ☐ **c.** Jack didn't give him a tip.

4. What did Jack learn about the United States?
   - ☐ **a.** It has a tipping culture.
   - ☐ **b.** You don't need to tip people.
   - ☐ **c.** It's tipping rules are similar to Singapore.

B *Listen to the conversation and fill in the blanks.* **CD** 2-07 WEB動画 🖥

Sheryl is at a restaurant in the United States with her friend Jack, who is visiting from Singapore.

Jack: That was a great meal! Let's grab our change and go.

Sheryl: Don't take all of that money. You have to leave a tip!

Jack: Oh, that's right. Will these coins be enough?

Sheryl: Not even [1]_____. In the United States, you should always tip between 15 and 20 percent of the total cost of the meal. The better the service, the [2]_____ the tip.

Jack: Well, I guess that should do it.

Sheryl: You do know that you don't just tip at restaurants, right?

Jack: What do you mean?

Sheryl: You should also tip taxi drivers about 15 percent of the [3]_____ and give them an extra dollar or two if they carry your bags.

Jack: I didn't know that. No [4]_____ the taxi driver seemed angry.

Sheryl: What about the hotel [5]_____? Did you tip him?

Jack: I gave him two dollars per bag. Was that OK?

Sheryl: That's fine. And don't forget the [6]_____. You should always leave a tip of three or four dollars on your [7]_____ or in the envelope that the hotel provides for that.

Jack: Wow! The United States really has a tipping culture. I'm going to go [8]_____!

C *Practice the conversation with your partner.*

DISCUSSION

D *Discuss the following with your classmates.*

1. Do you tip in your country?
2. Have you ever encountered any unfamiliar customs?

The + more/adj.-er + (S. + V.), the + more/adj.-er + (S. + V.)

we often omit the be verb in double comparatives

- The more comfortable the sofa (<u>is</u>),
  the more difficult it is to get up from it.

if the subject is not important, it can be omitted

- **The older** (the man is), **the wiser** (he will be).

- **The more** you practice, **the more** you will improve.

- **The more** sleep you get, **the better** you'll feel in the morning.

adj.-er and adj.-er
more and more + N.

Repeated comparatives are used to describe actions and things that are increasing or decreasing.

- The air in the city is getting
  <u>**dirtier and dirtier**</u>.

  adj.-er and adj.-er

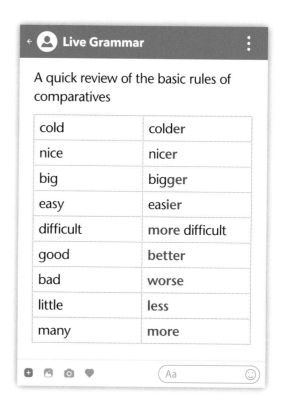

Live Grammar

A quick review of the basic rules of comparatives

cold	colder
nice	nicer
big	bigger
easy	easier
difficult	more difficult
good	better
bad	worse
little	less
many	more

Aa

more and more + N.

- As there are <u>**more and more cars**</u> in the city, air pollution will continue to increase.

Work It Out

Ⓐ *Check the correct answers.*

① (☐ More / ☐ The more) people you invite, (☐ the / ☐ ×) merrier we will feel.

② (☐ × / ☐ The) cheaper the dress is, (☐ the more / ☐ more) likely I am to buy it.

③ (☐ The longer / ☐ Longer) one's hair is, (☐ the / ☐ ×) more difficult it is to take care of.

④ (☐ Later / ☐ The later) you go to bed, (☐ the / ☐ ×) harder it is to wake up.

⑤ (☐ The more / ☐ The fewer) pieces the puzzle includes, (☐ the / ☐ ×) easier it becomes.

Ⓑ *Fill in the blanks with the hints given.*

① A: What time should we plan on arriving at the museum?

B: _____ (early, better). It can get very crowded by noon.

② English is an international language—that's why _____ (more) people are learning it.

③ If the temperature keeps increasing, it will get _____ (hot).

④ Debra became _____ (excited) as her wedding day approached.

⑤ That boy is growing _____ (tall) every day.

Ⓒ *Use the following sentence segments to create double comparatives of your own.*

① books / read / knowledge / gain

_____

② difficult / exam / students / fail

_____

③ people / come / food / need

_____

④ exercise / healthy / become

_____

⑤ money / spend / money / save

_____

Tips on Travel Etiquette

🎵 2-08

The more you travel, the more important it becomes to learn the customs of your destination country. Tipping is a great example of an important custom to master. In most European countries, tipping is appreciated but not expected. In the United States, it's rude not to tip workers like restaurant servers and
5 taxi drivers, as tips are an important part of their income. In Japan, it's just the opposite. Good service is considered absolutely important, so a happy customer is seen as the ideal reward.

Gift giving is another activity which varies around the world. It's considered good manners in the United States to open a gift as soon as it's received. That
10 way, the person giving it can share in the recipient's joy. But this is not the case in China or India, where gifts should be opened in private. The type of gift should also be carefully considered. For instance, a designer purse would be a welcome present for many people in many countries, but in Russia, giving someone an empty purse means you wish them financial ruin.

15 When traveling abroad, be aware of your hands and feet. In parts of the Middle East and South Asia, the bottoms of people's feet are considered dirty, so showing them is rude. The left hand is also considered unclean, so visitors must remember to avoid using their left hand whenever possible and to eat mostly with their right.

20 The key to adopting proper etiquette while abroad is to consider it part of the joy of traveling. Cultural differences are worth learning about, and they make the world a more interesting place. The more customs you learn, the more valuable your experience will be!

A *Fill in the blanks with the word choices given. Change the word form if necessary.*

> absolutely / reward / destination / financial / consider

1. Every time the dog did a trick, its owner gave it a _____.

2. Thomas lost his job, and his _____ situation right now isn't very good.

3. Emily is _____ Jamaica for her vacation.

4. The suitcase is _____ full, so you can't put anything else in it.

5. Jane will stop in Chicago, but New York is her final _____.

B *Check the correct answers.*

1. Where would a tip NOT be accepted?
   - ☐ **a.** In Japan
   - ☐ **b.** In the United States
   - ☐ **c.** In many European countries

2. In which country should you open a gift immediately?
   - ☐ **a.** India
   - ☐ **b.** China
   - ☐ **c.** The United States

3. Why is an empty purse a bad gift in Russia?
   - ☐ **a.** It means you want to take someone's money.
   - ☐ **b.** It means you wish someone good fortune.
   - ☐ **c.** It means you want someone to lose all their money.

4. What shouldn't you do in the Middle East?
   - ☐ **a.** Keep the bottom of your feet hidden
   - ☐ **b.** Eat with your left hand
   - ☐ **c.** Eat with your right hand

C *What are some other taboos in your country? Try to list them.*

_____

_____

_____

_____

_____

UNIT
08

CULTURE SHOCK

WRITING

What should a visitor to another country know about local customs? Help visitors to your country by preparing a list of dos and don'ts. Below are some tips to help you.

WORDS AND PHRASES

- greetings
- weather
- transportation in urban and suburban areas
- clothing / colors for special occasions
- food / eating in a restaurant
- eating out / tipping
- local people
- shopping

SENTENCE PATTERNS

- One of the most important things to remember is ...
- Another thing to keep in mind is ...
- One thing visitors don't often realize is ...
- Finally, you should never ...

When you visit my country, there ...

CHALLENGE YOURSELF

Part I Question & Response   🎧 2-09

Listen to the statement or question and choose the best response.

1. ☐ a   ☐ b   ☐ c   4. ☐ a   ☐ b   ☐ c
2. ☐ a   ☐ b   ☐ c   5. ☐ a   ☐ b   ☐ c
3. ☐ a   ☐ b   ☐ c

Part II Conversations   🎧 2-10

Listen to the conversation and answer the questions.

6. Why does the man take his shoes off?
   ☐ a. His feet hurt.
   ☐ b. They are very dirty.
   ☐ c. It's cooler that way.
   ☐ d. It's the tradition.

7. What is the man saying to the woman?
   ☐ a. He wants to break up with her.
   ☐ b. He's glad she's worried about him.
   ☐ c. He's concerned about her.
   ☐ d. He treats Amanda poorly.

8. What is the woman saying about Ashley and Alice?
   ☐ a. They are not really twins.
   ☐ b. They are both equally nice.
   ☐ c. They are completely different.
   ☐ d. They are both having twins.

9. Why didn't the man invite George?
   ☐ a. He didn't want to come.
   ☐ b. He didn't know George.
   ☐ c. He is too busy.
   ☐ d. George behaves badly.

10. What might be true about the woman?
   ☐ a. She is a student.
   ☐ b. She loves sweets.
   ☐ c. She is a teacher.
   ☐ d. She eats a lot of candy.

Linguaporta Training

Let's review the unit with Linguaporta.

93

School Activities

WARM UP

TALK ABOUT THIS

Talk about these questions.

Do you think you're qualified to be a class leader? Why or why not?

GEAR UP

A *Listen and look at the pictures below. What do you think is happening in each picture?* 🎧 2-11

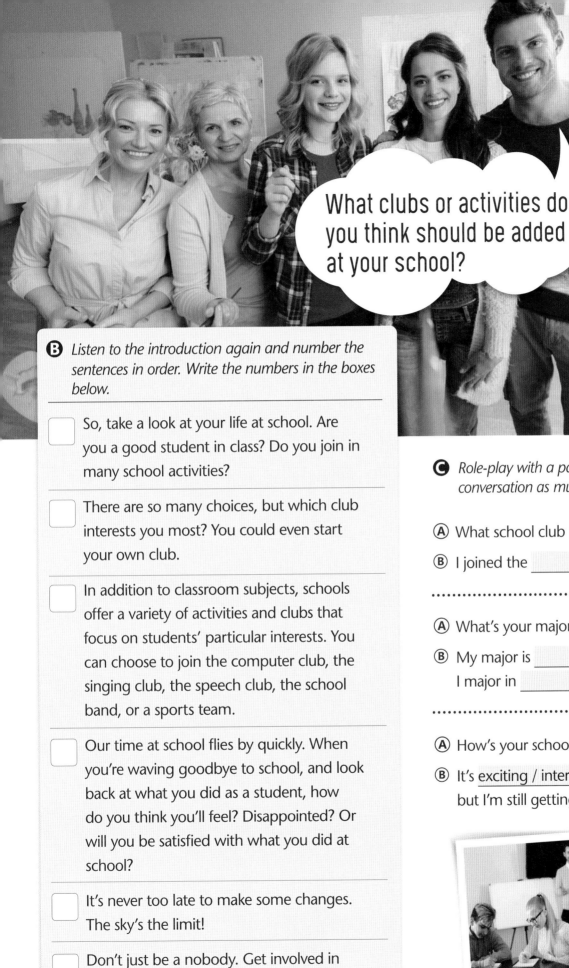

What clubs or activities do you think should be added at your school?

B *Listen to the introduction again and number the sentences in order. Write the numbers in the boxes below.*

☐ So, take a look at your life at school. Are you a good student in class? Do you join in many school activities?

☐ There are so many choices, but which club interests you most? You could even start your own club.

☐ In addition to classroom subjects, schools offer a variety of activities and clubs that focus on students' particular interests. You can choose to join the computer club, the singing club, the speech club, the school band, or a sports team.

☐ Our time at school flies by quickly. When you're waving goodbye to school, and look back at what you did as a student, how do you think you'll feel? Disappointed? Or will you be satisfied with what you did at school?

☐ It's never too late to make some changes. The sky's the limit!

☐ Don't just be a nobody. Get involved in something extra and you will soon get a good reputation on campus.

C *Role-play with a partner. Extend the conversation as much as you can.*

Ⓐ What school club did you join?

Ⓑ I joined the _____ .

· ·

Ⓐ What's your major?

Ⓑ My major is _____ . / I major in _____ .

· ·

Ⓐ How's your school life?

Ⓑ It's exciting / interesting / not bad, but I'm still getting used to it.

THE BENEFITS OF BEING A STUDENT

A *Watch the video clip and check the correct answers.* WEB動画 💻

1. How did Daniel find out about the night outing?
   ☐ **a.** He saw ads in a school magazine.
   ☐ **b.** His friend told him about it.
   ☐ **c.** He saw posters at school.

2. Who can join the night outing?
   ☐ **a.** Students that belong to Live and ABC University only
   ☐ **b.** Only students that do not belong to Live or ABC University
   ☐ **c.** Any university student who wishes to take part

3. Where does the event take place?
   ☐ **a.** At Live Park
   ☐ **b.** At ABC University
   ☐ **c.** At Live University

4. What do students need to join the night outing?
   ☐ **a.** They just need to bring money.
   ☐ **b.** They just need to bring a student ID.
   ☐ **c.** They do not need to bring anything.

B *Listen to the conversation and fill in the blanks.* 🎧 2-12 📺

Sally runs into Daniel on campus.

Sally: Hey, Daniel! I heard that Live University and ABC University are getting together for a night out next Friday night. Sounds interesting! Do you know about that?

Daniel: Yes! I've seen ¹_____ and posters everywhere at school and even on Facebook. My friends keep asking about it.

Sally: Your friends? You mean students that don't ²_____ to Live and ABC University can also come, too?

Daniel: Sure! It sounds like it'll be the biggest night out of the year, doesn't it?

Sally: Wow! That's fantastic! I'll ³_____ my friends for sure.

Daniel: Yeah, pretty cool! You know ⁴_____? It will be held at Live Park, and amazingly, they've even ⁵_____ a D.J. and an M.C.

Sally: Yeah, I know.

Daniel: Wait! Let me finish. It is totally free for students. Just bring your student ID. That's it.

Sally: ⁶_____! Being a student has its benefits. Hey, you will be there next Friday, won't you?

Daniel: For sure! I wouldn't ⁷_____ this night out for anything.

Sally: Great! Well, I'm ⁸_____ late for class.

Daniel: See you next week.

C *Practice the conversation with your partner.*

DISCUSSION

D *Discuss the following with your classmates.*

1. Do you ever attend after-school events?
2. Does your school hold dances and parties for students?
3. What benefits does your school offer students?

A tag question is a question that is added at the end of a sentence. It is used when the speaker is asking for confirmation. A positive statement is followed by a negative tag; a negative statement is followed by a positive tag.

> **S. + V., be/aux. + pron. ?**

• They are students, <u>aren't</u> **they?**
     +   **−**
   (positive statement)   *(negative tag)*

• You didn't play basketball last night, **did you?**
    −   **+**

• Mr. Green speaks Chinese fluently, **doesn't <u>he</u> ?**
     +   **−**

→ *use pronouns in question tags*

• The students have finished their homework, **haven't <u>they</u> ?**
      +   **−**

Tag questions can also be used to express intention.

• Let's go, **shall we?**

• Open the door, **will you?**

← 👤 **Live Grammar** ⋮

Statements with negative adverbs are NOT positive statements.

> hardly, scarcely, never, seldom, barely, rarely

• He seldom drinks coffee, does he?

➕ 🖼 📷 ♥   (Aa   ☺)

Work It Out

A *Check the correct answers.*

① You have a big family, (☐ haven't / ☐ aren't / ☐ don't) you?

② I can't borrow your car, (☐ will / ☐ can / ☐ shall) I?

③ All these shoes are yours, (☐ won't / ☐ aren't / ☐ don't) they?

④ You will come here, (☐ will / ☐ won't / ☐ do) you?

⑤ Let's move on to the next page, (☐ don't / ☐ shall / ☐ will) we?

B *Fill in the blanks with tag questions.*

① The concert is tonight, _____ ?

② Mrs. Lee can do it, _____ ?

③ You major in English, _____ ?

④ He often goes to the gym, _____ ?

⑤ Turn off the light, _____ ?

So/Neither + Be/Aux. + S.

So is used in affirmative sentences, and **neither** is used in negative sentences.

	Affirmatives	Negatives
Be Verb	Sean is American, and <u>Miranda is, too</u>. = Sean is American, and <u>so is</u> Miranda.	May isn't young, and <u>Jean isn't, either</u>. = May isn't young, <u>and **neither** is Jean</u>.
Auxiliary Verb (do, does, did)	Ben likes jogging, and <u>Nancy does, too</u>. = Ben likes jogging, and <u>so does Nancy</u>.	Pam didn't join a school club, and <u>Joe didn't, either</u>. = Pam didn't join a school club, and <u>**neither** did Joe</u>.
Auxiliary Verb (can, will, have, has, etc.)	I can play the piano, and <u>my sister can, too</u>. = I can play the piano, and <u>so can my sister</u>.	We haven't seen Diana for many years, and <u>they haven't, either</u>. = We haven't seen Diana for many years, and <u>**neither** have they</u>.

Work It Out

Combine the two sentences using **so** *or* **neither**.

① Joy's job doesn't pay well. / My job doesn't pay well, either.

_____

② I can run fast. / Melody can run fast, too.

_____

③ Danny didn't understand the vocabulary. / His older sister didn't understand it, either.

_____

④ I'll go on a trip next Sunday. / Sandy will go on a trip next Sunday, too.

_____

JOIN THE CLUB!

2-13

School clubs are becoming more and more popular in the United States. This is because they provide students with a number of benefits.

Being able to meet people with the same interests is one reason students join school clubs. They make it easier for them to find their place in school life.

5   Most clubs are cheap to join and require no special abilities. This makes them open to anyone and helps build several friendly and effective communities within the school.

Some students join a particular school club just so they have something to boost their résumés. What potential employer would not be impressed to see
10 that an interviewee has been a member of the debate club, or sign-language club, or English conversation club?

Parents and friends can pressure students to join a particular club. Unfortunately, this means that many clubs have memberships that consist of people who don't really want to be there. This is a waste of time and money for
15 the student and can spoil the atmosphere of the club.

To get the best out of school clubs, be careful about which ones you join. Choose ones that you know you will participate in. This way, you get more out of it, and so do your fellow club members.

A *Fill in the blanks with the word choices given. Change the word form if necessary.*

> require / spoil / atmosphere / particular / employer

1. This restaurant has a very romantic _____, so you should take your girlfriend there.

2. Many parents _____ their children by giving them everything they want.

3. Is there a(n) _____ kind of chocolate you want me to buy for you?

4. Many _____ are looking for people who are both creative and intelligent.

5. Plants _____ water and sunlight.

B *Check the correct answers.*

1. What's the main idea of the article?
   - ☐ **a.** To show the different kinds of clubs you can join at school
   - ☐ **b.** To talk about the benefits of joining a school club
   - ☐ **c.** To show how students join clubs for only the right reasons

2. Why do freshmen like to join school clubs?
   - ☐ **a.** They are able to get help with difficult homework projects.
   - ☐ **b.** It helps them to get comfortable with their new school.
   - ☐ **c.** It's a great way to meet people who have different interests.

3. What makes most school clubs easy to join?
   - ☐ **a.** They are cheap, and you don't need special skills.
   - ☐ **b.** They can help make résumés look better to an employer.
   - ☐ **c.** They help students meet people with different hobbies.

4. Why do some clubs have members who don't really want to be there?
   - ☐ **a.** They weren't very careful about the ones they joined.
   - ☐ **b.** They wasted a lot of their precious time and money.
   - ☐ **c.** They were pressured by friends and parents to join.

5. How can joining a school club help you get a good job?
   - ☐ **a.** It can help you meet future employers.
   - ☐ **b.** It can look quite good on your résumé.
   - ☐ **c.** It can help you get the most out of school.

What are the most important things when choosing a high school? Read the sample article and write a passage around 150 words.

Choosing the Right High School

Picking the right high school is the most important decision of my life so far. There are a few things I can keep in mind to help me make the best choice. First, it's all about the teachers. Teachers with a passion for education can inspire students to learn. Diversity is also a big deal. I want my teachers to come from a wide variety of backgrounds and cultures.

Second, I care a lot about my friends. If some of my friends choose a certain school, I might also choose that school so that I can be with them. In order to have fun and enjoy the social aspects of high school, I'd like to already have a few friends at school. Last of all, I prefer smaller class sizes. Smaller student-to-teacher ratios increase the attention each student gets. More attention means better teaching and a better chance to learn.

Part I Question & Response 🎧 2-14

Listen to the statement or question and choose the best response.

1. ☐ a ☐ b ☐ c
2. ☐ a ☐ b ☐ c
3. ☐ a ☐ b ☐ c

4. ☐ a ☐ b ☐ c
5. ☐ a ☐ b ☐ c

Part II Conversations 🎧 2-15

Listen to the conversation and answer the questions.

6. Why did the man take so many courses?
   ☐ a. He wanted to learn how to write a good résumé.
   ☐ b. He wanted to spoil his résumé.
   ☐ c. He wanted to help his brother.
   ☐ d. He wanted his résumé to look better.

7. How does the woman know about the movie club?
   ☐ a. She read an article about it.
   ☐ b. She used to be a member.
   ☐ c. She is a member.
   ☐ d. Her sister is a member.

8. What does the man say about his vacation?
   ☐ a. He feels like it was shorter than two months.
   ☐ b. He didn't really go on vacation.
   ☐ c. His airplane is up in the sky right now.
   ☐ d. He went on a vacation by airplane.

9. What is the woman doing to the man?
   ☐ a. She is helping him out.
   ☐ b. She is pressuring him.
   ☐ c. She is letting him finish.
   ☐ d. She is making him run late.

10. Why is the man preparing to make a speech?
   ☐ a. He is testing ideas for the debate club.
   ☐ b. He doesn't want people to play anymore.
   ☐ c. He is going to ask people to perform a play.
   ☐ d. He wants to get a part in a play.

Linguaporta Training

Let's review the unit with Linguaporta.

UNIT
09

SCHOOL ACTIVITIES

WARM UP

TALK ABOUT THIS
Talk about these questions.

> How do you usually find your way around in an unfamiliar place?

GEAR UP

 Listen to the short talks and choose the correct pictures. 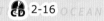 2-16

Question 1.

Question 2.

Have you ever got lost?
What happened?

B *Role-play with a partner. Extend the conversation as much as you can.*

Ⓐ Excuse me. Could you tell me how to get to the _____?

Ⓑ Go straight for _____ blocks and turn <u>right / left</u> at the traffic light. Then, you'll see it on your <u>right / left</u>.
....

Ⓐ Is there _____ around here?

Ⓑ Yes, there is. Turn <u>right / left</u> at the intersection and it'll be on your <u>right / left</u>.
....

Ⓐ What's the best way to get to the _____ from here?

Ⓑ Well, you could take a <u>taxi / bus</u>.

105

CONVERSATION

How Can We Get There?

A *Watch the video clip and check the correct answers.* WEB動画 🖥️

1. At first, which museum do Ben and Karen want to visit?
   - ☐ **a.** The Metropolitan Museum of Art
   - ☐ **b.** The Museum of the City of New York
   - ☐ **c.** The New York Museum of Modern Art

2. How long do Ben and Karen go around in circles?
   - ☐ **a.** For half an hour
   - ☐ **b.** For 10 minutes
   - ☐ **c.** For an hour

3. How will Ben and Karen most likely get to the museum?
   - ☐ **a.** On foot
   - ☐ **b.** By shuttle bus
   - ☐ **c.** By taxi

4. In the end, do Ben and Karen visit the museum they originally wanted to go to?
   - ☐ **a.** No, the museum is being rebuilt.
   - ☐ **b.** Yes, they go to the museum by taxi.
   - ☐ **c.** No, they're too exhausted to visit the museum.

106

Ben: These buildings look familiar. I think we just passed by here 10 minutes ago.

Karen: [1]_____ we're lost!

Ben: The boulevards, streets, and avenues are so [2]_____. We'll never find the museum!

Karen: Hey, stop complaining. How about asking someone else?

Ben: It seems like we have no other choice.

Karen asks a passing pedestrian.

Karen: Excuse me. Could you tell me how to get to the Metropolitan Museum of Art? We have [3]_____ around this area for an hour, but we still can't find it.

Man: It's in the opposite direction, and it's been under [4]_____ recently.

Ben: Oh, what bad luck! Can you suggest another place for us to visit?

Man: If you're [5]_____ of art, you may want to go to the Museum of the City of New York.

Ben: How do we get there?

Man: Walk along this street for 12 blocks and turn right when you see a green café. [6]_____ for six blocks more and then you'll see the museum on your right. You can take the [7]_____ bus if you like, but the bus stop is four blocks down the street.

Karen: I see. It sounds [8]_____, and we're exhausted. We should go there by taxi.

Ben: Thanks for your help.

Man: You're welcome. Have a nice trip.

C *Practice the conversation with your partner.*

DISCUSSION

D *Discuss the following with your classmates.*

1. Do you know the differences between boulevards, streets, and avenues?
2. What would you visit if you were in New York?
3. Do you think it's safe to take a taxi in an unfamiliar country?

UNIT
10

ASKING FOR DIRECTIONS

Participle Adjectives

*A participle is an adjective form from a verb. There are two types of participles: **-ing participles** and **-ed participles**.*

Participle Adjectives	Usage	-ed/-ing Adjectives
-ed Adjectives *(past participle: p.p.)*	Past participles usually end with **-ed, -d, -t, -en,** or **-n.** They are often used to describe how people feel about something or someone.	annoyed, bored, confused, excited, frustrated, frightened, satisfied, shocked, tired, interested, boiled, fallen
-ing Adjectives *(present participle: -ing)*	Present participles usually end with **-ing.** They are often used to describe something or someone.	annoying, boring, confusing, exciting, frustrating, frightening, satisfying, shocking, tiring, interesting, boiling, falling

- It's a **tiring** day for Sally.
- Sally was **tired** and went to bed early.

- The movie is **boring**.
- Jamie is **bored** with the movie.

Participle Phrases

Participle phrases are simplified by adjective clauses.

Active Voice

▶ *When it's an **active voice** sentence, we can delete the relative pronoun and be verb, and then change it to a **present participle** (V-ing).*

- Do you know the boy ~~who is~~ wearing a yellow jacket?
    - ➔ Do you know the boy <u>wearing a yellow jacket</u>?

- What is the name of the statue ~~that stands~~ in New York Harbor?
    - ➔ What is the name of the statue <u>standing in New York Harbor</u>?

Passive Voice

▶ *When it's a **passive voice** sentence, we can delete the relative pronoun and be verb, and then change it to a **past participle** (V-ed).*

- Sam is looking at a picture ~~that was~~ taken by a famous photographer.
    - ➔ Sam is looking at a picture <u>taken by a famous photographer.</u>

Work It Out

Ⓐ *Fill in the blanks based on the hints given.*

① The horror movie was very _____ (frighten).

② We were all _____ (shock) when we saw Sam's pink hair.

③ I became _____ (interest) in English when I was 15.

Ⓑ *Rewrite the following sentences using a participle phrase.*

① Kelly wore a sweater that had been made by her grandmother.

_____

② The man who is working in the yard is my father.

_____

③ There are many expensive bikes which are stolen every day.

_____

④ Last week, the Smiths moved into a house that faces the lake.

_____

GRAMMAR	**2 Participle Construction**

The participle construction is simplified by an adverb clause.

┌→ *1. delete the same pronoun   2. use present participle*

• Before ~~I go~~ grocery shopping, I make a list of the things we need.

→ <u>Before going grocery shopping</u>, I make a list of the things we need.

┌→ *1. delete the subordinate conjunction, the be verb, and the same pronoun   2. use past participle*

• ~~Because Shelly was~~ locked out of the house, ~~she~~ couldn't get her purse.

→ <u>Locked out of the house</u>, Shelly couldn't get her purse.

Work It Out

Rewrite the following sentences using a participle construction.

① After she did the dishes, Mandy made some tea.

_____, Mandy made some tea.

② Before he cleaned his room, Johnny did the laundry.

_____, Johnny did the laundry.

③ While we watched TV, we ate dinner.

_____, we ate dinner.

④ Because Bill was caught in a shower, he got soaked to the skin.

_____, Bill got soaked to the skin.

KEEPING FROM GETTING LOST

CD 2-18

Getting lost in an unfamiliar town can be scary. You can have difficulties reading signs or getting directions, and you could wind up in a bad neighborhood. But, with a little preparation, exploring a new city can be safe and full of adventure.

Learn all about the place you visit. Read a guidebook and ask at your hotel. Above all,
5   find out which areas you should avoid.

When going out, carry traveler's checks (which can be replaced if lost), a map or travel guide, and your hotel's business card. Also, carry some emergency cash in the local currency, and be sure to leave your passport and an emergency credit card or some traveler's checks in the hotel safe.

10   If you lose your way, try not to look like a lost tourist. Wearing a camera around your neck and worriedly studying a map will make you an easy target.

When asking for directions or help, think about who you should ask. Ask in a shop or a restaurant, or, if possible, ask a police officer. Bilingual phrase books are helpful; if you cannot say a phrase, you at least can point to it.

15   Exploring a new city can be a great adventure, but safety comes first. With a little planning and thought, sightseeing can be as safe as it is fun.

A *Fill in the blanks with the word choices given. Change the word form if necessary.*

> explore / adventure / replace / emergency / currency

1. The _____ in the U.S. is the dollar, while in Great Britain it is the pound.

2. Our office should buy new chairs to _____ these old ones.

3. Your three-month trip through India sounds like a great _____.

4. You will need lights and rope if you are going to _____ those caves.

5. Leo had a family _____, so he couldn't come to school today.

B *Check the correct answers.*

1. Which of these ideas is NOT mentioned as a good way to keep from getting lost?
   - ☐ **a.** Carry lots of money
   - ☐ **b.** Read a guidebook
   - ☐ **c.** Ask at your hotel

2. When going out in an unfamiliar city, what should you carry?
   - ☐ **a.** Your passport and an emergency credit card
   - ☐ **b.** Some traveler's checks and a hotel safe
   - ☐ **c.** A map and your hotel's business card

3. If you lose your way, which of the following actions is NOT suggested in the article?
   - ☐ **a.** Ask someone and point at the place in a bilingual phrase book
   - ☐ **b.** Ask a police officer for some help with directions
   - ☐ **c.** Study a map worriedly and get some money out

4. According to the article, who should you ask for help?
   - ☐ **a.** Someone in a restaurant or shop
   - ☐ **b.** Another traveler on the street
   - ☐ **c.** Anyone who has a book

5. At the end of the article, what does the writer think is most important?
   - ☐ **a.** Fun
   - ☐ **b.** Safety
   - ☐ **c.** Excitement

WRITING

Look at the pictures. What happened to the couple? Write a passage around 150 words.

CHALLENGE YOURSELF

Part I Question & Response   🎧 2-19

Listen to the statement or question and choose the best response.

1. ☐ a ☐ b ☐ c   4. ☐ a ☐ b ☐ c
2. ☐ a ☐ b ☐ c   5. ☐ a ☐ b ☐ c
3. ☐ a ☐ b ☐ c

Part II Conversations   🎧 2-20

Listen to the conversation and answer the questions.

6. What did the woman almost hit?
   - ☐ a. An animal
   - ☐ b. A person
   - ☐ c. A building
   - ☐ d. A tree

7. Why are they going to take a taxi?
   - ☐ a. The man can't contact Ken.
   - ☐ b. They don't want to be late to meet Ken.
   - ☐ c. The neighborhood is not very safe.
   - ☐ d. Ken's directions aren't clear enough.

8. What does the man say about the road?
   - ☐ a. It's being repaired.
   - ☐ b. There's a flood.
   - ☐ c. There's a car accident.
   - ☐ d. The traffic is heavy.

9. What happened to the man and woman?
   - ☐ a. They can't get a taxi until later.
   - ☐ b. They lost the map during their walk.
   - ☐ c. They're walking completely away from their destination.
   - ☐ d. They're out of food and water.

10. What will the woman do in the city?
    - ☐ a. Make plans
    - ☐ b. Do research
    - ☐ c. Travel around
    - ☐ d. Visit a friend

Linguaporta Training

Let's review the unit with Linguaporta.

WARM UP

TALK ABOUT THIS
Talk about these questions.

> What things do you consider important to take with you when you travel?

GEAR UP

 Listen to the conversations and choose the correct pictures. 🔊 2-21

Question 1.	Question 2.

Which country has the best food? How about shopping, sightseeing, and historical places?

Question 3.

B *Role-play with a partner. Extend the conversation as much as you can.*

Ⓐ Are you excited about your trip?

Ⓑ I can't wait! / No, I've been there many times.

....

Ⓐ Did you remember <u>your passport / camera / money / credit card?</u>

Ⓑ <u>Yes, I did. / No, I forgot it.</u>

....

Ⓐ How many bags will you be bringing?

Ⓑ [_____] check-in and [_____] carry-on.

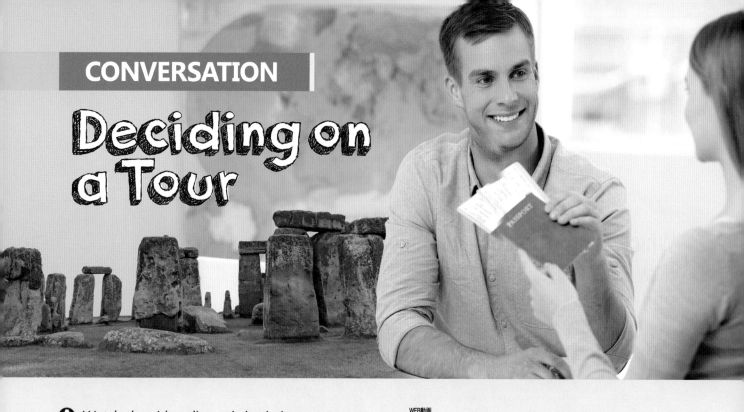

CONVERSATION

Deciding on a Tour

Ⓐ *Watch the video clip and check the correct answers.* WEB動画 🖥️

1. Which location does the travel agent NOT recommend to John?

☐ **a.** Paris

☐ **b.** The U.K.

☐ **c.** Africa

2. What does John want to do in the United Kingdom?

☐ **a.** Take a theater tour

☐ **b.** Go on an exciting safari

☐ **c.** See the major attractions

3. How long is the Royal Treasures Package?

☐ **a.** Four days

☐ **b.** Sixteen days

☐ **c.** Twelve days

4. How does John feel about the tour?

☐ **a.** He thinks it's too short.

☐ **b.** He thinks it's too expensive.

☐ **c.** He thinks the hotels aren't very nice.

116

B *Listen to the conversation and fill in the blanks.* 🎧 2-22 🖥️

John is at a travel agency.

Travel Agent: Where would you like to go, Mr. Smith? Paris is great this time of year. Or maybe an exciting tour in Africa is more your style.

John: Actually, I've always wanted to go to the United Kingdom. The summer ^1_____ from school is coming up, so it's the perfect time to go.

Travel Agent: We have several tour ^2_____ to the U.K. Let's see ... There are tours for theater, food, greatest sights, or ...

John: Well, since it's my first time there, I would like to see the major attractions.

Travel Agent: Great. The Royal Treasures Package is a 12-day tour that starts August 16. Upon arriving, you'll visit several sights in London. You'll also travel outside the ^3_____ to visit Shakespeare's home, Stonehenge, and the castle of King Arthur.

John: Tell me about meals. Are those ^4_____, too?

Travel Agent: A continental breakfast is provided every morning, but you're on your own for lunch and dinner. Also, tips for local guides are not included.

John: Wow! I'm ^5_____ about the price.

Travel Agent: It's an amazing price at $6,999. That includes airfare from New York, entrance ^6_____, travel within the country, and 4-star hotel accommodations every night. A $25 ^7_____ to use for room service, a spa treatment, or minibar refreshments is also included.

John: Well, I definitely feel like I'm being ^8_____!

C *Practice the conversation with your partner.*

DISCUSSION

D *Discuss the following with your classmates.*

1. Where do you most want to travel?
2. Is it better to use a travel agency or plan a trip yourself?
3. Do you like to travel off the beaten path?

UNIT
11

TOURIST SPOTS

117

GRAMMAR ☐1 Exclamatory Sentences

Exclamatory sentences end in exclamation marks (!) and indicate the strong feelings of the speaker.

> **What** + (a/an) + **Adj.** + **N.** + (S. + V.)!

✓ What a lovely
   young lady!

- What a great idea!
- What beautiful eyes she has!

> **How** + **Adj./Adv.** + (S. + V.)!

✓ How cute these
   dogs are!

- How lucky I am to have such a great friend!
- How fast he walks!

Work It Out

Rewrite the following sentences as exclamatory sentences.

① It was a very hot day.

_____

② The novel is very interesting.

_____

③ These puppies are so cute.

_____

④ Your sister has a very lovely smile.

_____

⑤ He's a very handsome man.

_____

⑥ The movie is so exciting.

_____

GRAMMAR ☐2 On/Upon + N./V-ing, S. + V.

> **On/Upon** + **N./V-ing**, **S.** + **V.**
> = **As soon as** + **S.** + **V.,** **S.** + **V.**
> = **The moment/minute/instant** + **S.** + **V.,** **S.** + **V.**

- **Upon completing** the task, <u>the students</u> <u>took</u> a break for lunch.

- **Upon arrival,** <u>the people</u> on the train <u>started</u> gathering their belongings.

- **Upon entering** the room, <u>Mike</u> <u>was greeted</u> by his dog.
  = As soon as Mike entered the room, he was greeted by his dog.

Work It Out

Rewrite the sentences based on the hints given.

① After my graduation from college, I went off to look for a job. (Upon + V-ing)

_____

② Upon hearing the good news, I called my best friend on the telephone. (As soon as)

_____

③ The party can start once Julia arrives with the birthday cake. (The moment)

_____

GRAMMAR   3 It is said that ...

It is said that + S. + V.
= People/They say + (that) + S. + V.
= S. + is/are said to + V.

- **It is said that** having a pet is good for a person's mental health.
  = **People say that** having a pet is good for a person's mental health.
  = Having a pet **is said to** be good for a person's mental health.

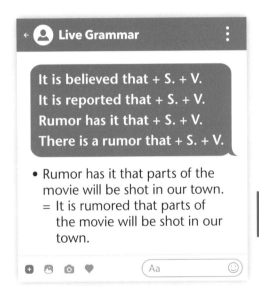

← 👤 **Live Grammar**   ⋮

It is believed that + S. + V.
It is reported that + S. + V.
Rumor has it that + S. + V.
There is a rumor that + S. + V.

- Rumor has it that parts of the movie will be shot in our town.
  = It is rumored that parts of the movie will be shot in our town.

⊕ 🎬 📷 ♥   (Aa   ☺)

UNIT
11

TOURIST SPOTS

Work It Out

Rewrite the sentences based on the hints given.

① It is said that this house is the home of a famous movie star. (People believe)

_____

② The snow is said to have stopped late last night. (It is said that)

_____

③ It is rumored that the company is being sold to a Japanese firm. (Rumor has it)

_____

Monuments to Love

2-23

Aristotle is believed to have said, "Love consists of a single soul inhabiting two bodies." When those two people find each other and the soul is reunited, anything is possible. In fact, some of the world's most incredible works are the result.

5   One of the most famous monuments to love is India's Taj Mahal. Upon the death of his favorite wife in the early 1600s, the emperor Shah Jahan built this amazing structure. The center building shines in white marble, a symbol of the purity of the emperor's love.

In Thailand, one of the most important temples has a romantic legend
10 behind it. Long ago, a prince fell deeply in love with a woman. Before they could marry, the prince was killed by a jealous enemy. It is said that the sad lover built a temple in Phimai, where she stayed to pray for the return of her prince's soul.

Another monument to love can be found in England. In 1290, the English
15 king Edward I's dear wife Eleanor died. It took twelve days to transport her body to its final resting place in London. At each nightly stop along the route, Edward built a huge stone cross in memory of his great love.

Much more recently, in 1993, a love monument was unveiled in Lima, Peru. For a new park, an artist created a huge statue showing a kiss with his wife.
20 There is now an annual contest: whichever couple can hold the pose of the statue the longest wins!

The power of love is incredible, and because of it, we have amazing monuments, castles, and artwork. Whether we're sharing a treat with a boyfriend or building a castle for a wife, love moves us.

A *Fill in the blanks with the word choices given. Change the word form if necessary.*

> jealous / enemy / pray / monument / incredible

1. The dancers do some _____ moves during the show.

2. The Statue of Liberty is one of the most famous _____ in the United States.

3. Mike has a great job, but I'm not _____ of him.

4. That country was our _____ in the war.

5. Every night, Jerry _____ before he goes to bed.

B *Check the correct answers.*

1. Who built the Taj Mahal?
   - ☐ a. Aristotle
   - ☐ b. An emperor in India
   - ☐ c. Shah Jahan's wife

2. Why was the temple built in Thailand?
   - ☐ a. It was built to honor the lives of a prince and princess.
   - ☐ b. A man built it to remember the soul of his lover.
   - ☐ c. A woman built it to pray for the return of her prince's soul.

3. When did Edward I's wife pass away?
   - ☐ a. 1290
   - ☐ b. 1993
   - ☐ c. The 1600s

4. How did Edward I honor his wife?
   - ☐ a. He built huge statues in her memory.
   - ☐ b. He built huge temples in her memory.
   - ☐ c. He built huge stone crosses in her memory.

5. How can you win the contest in Peru?
   - ☐ a. By holding a statue as long as you can
   - ☐ b. By creating a statue that resembles that one created by the artist
   - ☐ c. By holding the statue's pose longer than anyone else

Where is your hometown? How would you introduce it to your friends? Please write a passage around 150 words.

_____

_____

_____

_____

_____

_____

_____

_____

_____

_____

_____

_____

CHALLENGE YOURSELF

Listen to the statement or question and choose the best response.

1. ☐ a   ☐ b   ☐ c   4. ☐ a   ☐ b   ☐ c
2. ☐ a   ☐ b   ☐ c   5. ☐ a   ☐ b   ☐ c
3. ☐ a   ☐ b   ☐ c

Part II Conversations CD 2-25

Listen to the conversation and answer the questions.

6. What does the girl tell the man to see?
   ☐ a. The important structures that have history
   ☐ b. The famous museums that are free to enter
   ☐ c. The politicians working in the city
   ☐ d. The old restaurants that serve the best food

7. What does the man say about the broken mirror?
   ☐ a. The mirror can be fixed easily.
   ☐ b. He has one just like it in his bathroom.
   ☐ c. Looking in it is bad luck.
   ☐ d. People won't really get bad luck from it.

8. What is true about the floor?
   ☐ a. It feels the same as carpet.
   ☐ b. It looks see-through, like glass.
   ☐ c. It is made out of wood.
   ☐ d. It is smooth and made of stone.

9. What will the woman do?
   ☐ a. Check with another airplane company
   ☐ b. Change the date of travel
   ☐ c. Think about traveling somewhere else
   ☐ d. Change the destination

10. What is the man saying to the woman?
   ☐ a. His wife is in Europe.
   ☐ b. He had a really good time.
   ☐ c. His wife is a tour guide.
   ☐ d. He is feeling really tired.

UNIT
11

TOURIST SPOTS

Linguaporta Training

Let's review the unit with Linguaporta.

WARM UP

TALK ABOUT THIS

Talk about these questions.

> Have you thought about studying abroad? Why might you want to? Why not?

GEAR UP

A *Listen and look at the pictures below. What do you think is happening in each picture?* 2-26

Do you think people who have studied abroad get better job opportunities? Discuss your views.

B *Listen to the introduction again and number the sentences in order. Write the numbers in the boxes below.*

☐ Living in a new country and new culture might affect you in ways you don't expect.

☐ Studying in a foreign country is a serious decision. It can be a rewarding experience, but think carefully about how it will fit into your long-term educational and life plans.

☐ You may need to make some readjustments when you return home. It's also wise to think about how the move will impact you and also your family.

☐ Studying abroad is not for everyone, but if you think you can immerse yourself in a foreign culture for a year or more, the rewards are abundant.

☐ Think about the cost of education, including the cost of tuition, living expenses, books, and other items. Tuition varies widely from school to school, but it is almost always the biggest single cost that an international student has to face.

C *Role-play with a partner. Extend the conversation as much as you can.*

Ⓐ Do you want to study abroad?

Ⓑ Yes, I want to study in
_____ . / No, because
_____ .

••

Ⓐ What do you know about
_____ ?

Ⓑ I don't know much about that country. / Oh, that's a nice country. It's _____ .

••

Ⓐ What are some pros and cons of studying abroad?

Ⓑ Well, _____ .

UNIT
12

STUDYING ABROAD

A Welcome Dinner

A *Watch the video clip and check the correct answers.* WEB動画 🖥

1. What do we know about Pam?
   - ☐ **a.** She is a host.
   - ☐ **b.** She is a student.
   - ☐ **c.** She wants to become an American.

2. What does Pam say about Thailand?
   - ☐ **a.** There are few differences between American and Thai food cultures.
   - ☐ **b.** Rice and noodle dishes are becoming less popular in Thailand.
   - ☐ **c.** People in Thailand are influenced by American culture.

3. What does Arthur say about night markets?
   - ☐ **a.** He has never been to one.
   - ☐ **b.** They are uncommon.
   - ☐ **c.** They are strange.

4. Why does Pam apply to the language school in the United States?
   - ☐ **a.** She wants to experience American culture.
   - ☐ **b.** She has family living in the United States.
   - ☐ **c.** She picked a country at random.

B *Listen to the conversation and fill in the blanks.* 🎧 2-27 📺 WEB動画

Pam has just arrived for a homestay in the United States. She is enjoying a welcome dinner with her hosts, Arthur and Marion.

Arthur: Hope you like the food, Pam! By the way, what do you usually eat in Thailand?

Pam: Rice and noodle dishes are very ¹_____, but Thailand has become quite international in ²_____ of cuisine. These days, all kinds of foods are available there.

Marion: Oh, so perhaps you're ³_____ to American-style dishes. There must be some differences between the food cultures of the United States and Thailand, though.

Pam: There certainly are! I've heard that you don't have any night markets here.

Arthur: Right, they're ⁴_____ here—usually just for special occasions. Apart from the food, how do you like it here so far?

Pam: Well, there is one thing I find ⁵_____.

Arthur: What's that?

Pam: I don't understand why people keep their shoes on in the house. In Thailand, we always ⁶_____ them.

Marion: Oh, it's really a matter of ⁷_____. It's optional. So, I'm curious—why did you apply to language school in the United States rather than somewhere else?

Pam: Actually, I've always wanted to visit. In Thailand, we're often ⁸_____ by American culture, so I wanted to experience it for myself.

C *Practice the conversation with your partner.*

DISCUSSION

D *Discuss the following in a group.*

1. Have you had a homestay experience before?
2. Have you ever had a rude guest stay in your house? Talk about it.
3. What would you consider rude behavior from a guest staying in your home?

Conjunctive adverbs are used to join two independent clauses. Conjunctive adverbs show cause and effect, sequence, contrast, comparison, or other relationships.

> **Main clause**; + **conjunctive adverb**, + **main clause**.

To Express Cause and Effect

therefore, thus, hence, accordingly, as a result, consequently

- I don't like his suggestion; <u>therefore</u>, I won't help.

  in this sentence, there is a semicolon (;) before the conjunctive adverb (therefore) and a comma (,) after "therefore"

- Tim stayed up all night studying. **As a result**, he didn't wake up on time and missed his final.

  in this example, the conjunctive adverb (as a result) is at the beginning of a sentence, so we add a comma (,) after "as a result"

To Express Contrast

however, nevertheless, still, on the contrary, by contrast, instead, on the one hand, on the other hand

- I feel a bit tired. **However**, I can hang on.

- There is probably no serious damage; **nevertheless**, it is better to check and make sure.

To Express Addition

besides, moreover, also, furthermore, in addition, what's more

- To stay healthy, you need a balanced diet and regular exercise. **In addition**, you should have a routine physical checkup.

To Express Conclusion

all in all, in a word, in short, in brief, in sum, in conclusion

- The food was good, the music was fantastic, and the host was funny. **All in all**, I'd say that the party was a success.

Work It Out

A *Fill in the blanks with the words in the box.*

moreover / however / in short / as a result

① Gary looked weak; _____, he insisted on going to work.

② We had circled around this area for an hour, and the roads all looked the same. _____, we were lost.

③ It's OK if you don't have time to meet me. _____, it's late and rainy outside.

④ The store had been full all day long, and customers lined up for their food. _____, the store made a lot of money.

B *Add commas, semicolons, or periods as needed. If you add a period, make the next letter a capital. Do not add other connecting words.*

① John refused to apply for a job however he pretended to look for one.

_____

_____

② The car had engine trouble consequently we arrived later than planned.

_____

_____

③ I have to work hard at math nevertheless I enjoy the subject.

_____

_____

④ My father does not go to sports events or concerts instead he watches them on television.

_____

_____

⑤ My mother works as an accountant and real estate agent also she sometimes does some interior decorating.

_____

_____

⑥ Nick was mean to his co-workers therefore no one wanted to help him when he was in trouble.

_____

_____

Homestay Etiquette

2-28

If you are going abroad to study, a homestay provides a fun, eye-opening experience that an ordinary college dorm just can't match. In a dorm, you will meet fellow students from foreign countries, but you will be mostly on your own. On the other hand, in a homestay, a family opens up their home to you,
5 presenting a unique window into everyday life in that country.

You will want to make your homestay a pleasant one, so there are certain rules of etiquette you should follow. Of course, you'll make a good first impression if you arrive with some small gifts for your hosts—something unique to your country will be much appreciated. Even though you will be told to make
10 yourself at home, ask about house rules and always respect them.

During your stay, keep your bedroom tidy, and always clean up after yourself, especially in the bathroom. Offer to do the dishes and your own laundry. If you need to use the telephone, be sure to ask first. When you go out, it's a good idea to tell your host family where you are going and what time they can expect
15 you back, so they won't worry about you.

Numerous organizations matching students to welcoming families worldwide have listings on the Internet. In addition, if you are going abroad for a language program, a homestay will give you real-life language practice above and beyond that which you'll receive in the classroom. So if you are studying overseas,
20 consider a homestay.

A *Fill in the blanks with the word choices given. Change the word form if necessary.*

> laundry / provide / abroad / addition / ordinary

1. That looks like a(n) _____ house, but it's actually a museum.

2. Chris has lived _____ for many years.

3. Every Saturday, Kenny does the _____ and then folds all of the clean clothes.

4. All meals are _____ at no additional cost.

5. Betty can speak English. In _____, she can speak French and Japanese.

B *Check the correct answers.*

1. What's the difference between a college dorm and a homestay?
   - ☐ a. In a college dorm, there is no need to follow any rules.
   - ☐ b. In a homestay, you'll gain an eye-opening experience.
   - ☐ c. In a homestay, you'll have more windows in your room.

2. According to the article, when is a good time to give small gifts to your hosts?
   - ☐ a. After you leave your host family's home
   - ☐ b. When you finish doing the dishes and your own laundry
   - ☐ c. When you arrive at your host family's home

3. What kind of gifts will be most liked by your host family?
   - ☐ a. Something useful from your country
   - ☐ b. Something that comes from your parents' home
   - ☐ c. Something unique from your own country

4. During your stay, what should you pay attention to?
   - ☐ a. Always help with household chores
   - ☐ b. Never use the telephone
   - ☐ c. Clean up the house every day

5. When you go out, you should tell your host family _____.
   - ☐ a. when you're going back to your country
   - ☐ b. where you're planning to go
   - ☐ c. what time you're leaving the house

C *Write down your answers.*

1. Have you ever stayed at a host family abroad?

_____

2. Would you like to stay with a host family? If yes, when and where?

_____

UNIT
12

STUDYING ABROAD

131

WRITING

What would your ideal host couple be like? Fill out the application form to request a homestay and write four to five sentences about your ideal host couple. Then, read your sentences to your classmates.

Place your request: ☐ U.S.A. ☐ U.K. ☐ Canada ☐ Australia

First name: _____

Last name: _____

Country: _____

City: _____

Age: _____ **Gender:** ☐ Female ☐ Male

E-mail: _____

The homestay you are looking for ...

Destination: _____ **City:** _____

How much are you willing to pay? (U.S.$ / month): _____

Period from: _____ **to:** _____

Purpose of trip: ☐ Learn language ☐ Learn culture ☐ Tourism ☐ Business

Do you smoke? ☐ Yes ☐ No

Do you want meals included? ☐ Yes ☐ No ☐ Do not care

Are you allergic to animals? ☐ Yes ☐ No ☐ Do not care

Please include additional information or comments about yourself and the purpose of your stay:

_____

_____

_____

_____

_____

_____

CHALLENGE YOURSELF

Listen to the statement or question and choose the best response.

1. ☐ a   ☐ b   ☐ c   4. ☐ a   ☐ b   ☐ c
2. ☐ a   ☐ b   ☐ c   5. ☐ a   ☐ b   ☐ c
3. ☐ a   ☐ b   ☐ c

Part II   Conversations   🎧 2-30

Listen to the conversation and answer the questions.

6. How did the woman describe her vacation?
   ☐ a. It was very tiring.
   ☐ b. It was too short.
   ☐ c. It was boring.
   ☐ d. It was enjoyable.

7. What does Marie tell Joe to do?
   ☐ a. Help her make the dinner
   ☐ b. Relax and be comfortable
   ☐ c. Set the table for her
   ☐ d. Clean up the kitchen

8. Who has the man invited over?
   ☐ a. Some of his neighbors
   ☐ b. Some people he met at a party
   ☐ c. Some of his co-workers
   ☐ d. Some people who he works for

9. What does the man say about the server?
   ☐ a. He had bad manners.
   ☐ b. He kept making mistakes.
   ☐ c. He spilled something on the man.
   ☐ d. He served some very cold food.

10. What does the man tell the woman to do?
   ☐ a. Go online to list his apartment for rent
   ☐ b. Make a list of apartments she likes
   ☐ c. Put herself on a list to look for a roommate
   ☐ d. Look through lists of apartment rentals online

UNIT
12

STUDYING ABROAD

Linguaporta Training

Let's review the unit with Linguaporta.

Review 2

Listen to the statement or question and check the best response.

1. ☐ a   ☐ b   ☐ c   3. ☐ a   ☐ b   ☐ c
2. ☐ a   ☐ b   ☐ c   4. ☐ a   ☐ b   ☐ c

Part II 🎵 2-32

Listen to the conversation and check the correct answer.

1. What does Sandy say that Ron can do?
   ☐ a. Go to the movies
   ☐ b. Write the speech
   ☐ c. Join the student association
   ☐ d. Rely on her

2. Where is the Star Hotel?
   ☐ a. Across from a bank
   ☐ b. Kitty-corner from a movie theather
   ☐ c. Between a movie theather and a bank
   ☐ d. Two blocks away

3. Why is Pearl joining the student newspaper?
   ☐ a. She's a great writer.
   ☐ b. She loves accounting.
   ☐ c. It'll help her get a job.
   ☐ d. She can write fluff pieces.

4. What did Katy do?
   ☐ a. She gave Steven information about Australia.
   ☐ b. She put a souvenir on Steven's desk.
   ☐ c. She gave Steven sugar for his coffee.
   ☐ d. She returned Steven's coffee cup.

Part III 🎵 2-33

Listen to the short passage and check the correct picture.

1.

 ☐ a    ☐ b    ☐ c

2.

 ☐ a    ☐ b    ☐ c

Part IV

Fill in the blanks.

> participated in / laundry / exhausted / benefits / particular
> explore / currency / monuments / accommodations / occasion

1. Tony _____ many club activities to spice up his college life.

2. After hearing the _____ of the plan, I agreed to help.

3. Is there a _____ movie that you want to see tonight?

4. Make sure you have some local _____ with you when you travel abroad.

5. After running the marathon, Alec was _____.

6. Every weekend, I try to _____ a different part of the city.

7. We visited the major _____ when we went to London.

8. When I arrived in the city, I immediately started looking for _____ for the night.

9. This wine is for a special _____.

10. Do you have any clothes that need to be washed? I'm doing the _____ now.

Part V

Check the correct answer.

1. _____ a little preparation, exploring a new city can be safe and full of adventure.
   ☐ **a.** With   ☐ **b.** To   ☐ **c.** For   ☐ **d.** Toward

2. A: You don't like fast food, _____?
   B: Actually, I do. I like hamburgers and French fries very much.
   ☐ **a.** are you   ☐ **b.** do you   ☐ **c.** aren't you   ☐ **d.** don't you

3. Her name is known _____ everybody.
   ☐ **a.** as   ☐ **b.** for   ☐ **c.** in   ☐ **d.** to

4. _____ uncomfortable, my father went to our family doctor this morning.
   ☐ **a.** To feel   ☐ **b.** Feel   ☐ **c.** Not felt   ☐ **d.** Feeling

5. Why don't we have our house _____ this summer?
   ☐ **a.** paint   ☐ **b.** painted   ☐ **c.** painting   ☐ **d.** to paint

6. Rose wants to get her kids _____ more vegetables.
   ☐ **a.** eat   ☐ **b.** ate   ☐ **c.** to eat   ☐ **d.** eaten

7. Little _____ that Jack would lie.
   ☐ **a.** we believe   ☐ **b.** we did believed   ☐ **c.** did we believed   ☐ **d.** did we believe

8. The more people you invite, _____ we will feel.
   ☐ **a.** merrier   ☐ **b.** more merry   ☐ **c.** the merrier   ☐ **d.** the more merry

9. Helen's parents do not allow her _____ out past 10:00 p.m.
   ☐ **a.** to stay   ☐ **b.** stay   ☐ **c.** staying   ☐ **d.** stays

10. The chairman refused _____ any more questions.
    ☐ **a.** to answer   ☐ **b.** answering   ☐ **c.** to answering   ☐ **d.** answered

Read the article and check the correct answer.

Across the world, there are famous landmarks that are easily recognized. These include buildings, statues, and bridges, and many of them have interesting histories.

In Paris, the Eiffel Tower is among the most visited landmarks in the world. The 324-meter iron tower was built for the 1889 World's Fair. It was almost torn down in 1909 but was kept as
5   a radiotelegraph station to gather information from enemies during World War I. In the midst of World War II, the Eiffel Tower narrowly avoided destruction again. Hitler told soldiers to destroy the tower, which had become an icon of France. Luckily, his orders were never followed.

Another world-famous landmark is New York's Statue of Liberty. The bronze statue of a goddess holding a torch and a tablet was designed by French sculptor Frédéric Bartholdi. The
10 monument of freedom was given to the United States by the people of France to remember the American Revolution. Many believe that the crown's seven spikes are for the seven continents of the world, representing global freedom.

Besides towers and statues, bridges are also popular landmarks. One of the most famous is Tower Bridge in London, completed in 1894. A public competition was held to design the
15 bridge, and eventually a <u>drawbridge</u> was chosen, as it opens to allow tall ships to pass through. Ships have priority, [   ] cars must wait for passing boats. Even former U.S. president Bill Clinton was stopped by the bridge when he visited London in 1997, to the dismay of his separated security team. There's a story behind every landmark. Next time you have a chance to visit one, perhaps you can find out how and why it was built.

1. Which sentence is true about the Eiffel Tower?
- ☐ **a.** It was torn down during World War II.
- ☐ **b.** It was used as a radiotelegraph station during World War I.
- ☐ **c.** Hitler ordered his soldiers not to destroy the tower.

2. French sculptor Frédéric Bartholdi designed the statue of a goddess holding _____.
- ☐ **a.** a crown
- ☐ **b.** a torch
- ☐ **c.** a torch and a tablet

3. The underlined word "drawbridge" means a bridge that can _____ in order to allow big boats to go under it.
- ☐ **a.** be pulled up
- ☐ **b.** be torn down
- ☐ **c.** disappear

4. The word that belongs in the [   ] in this article is _____.
- ☐ **a.** so
- ☐ **b.** because
- ☐ **c.** but

5. What is the best title for this article?

☐ **a.** The Story Behind the Eiffel Tower

☐ **b.** Landmarks That Are Hardly Recognized

☐ **c.** Discovering the History of Landmarks

Part VII

Read the following hint and write a paragraph in 80-120 words.

Have you ever encountered culture shock? What are some culture differences among countries? Share your experience or opinion.

_____

_____

_____

_____

_____

_____

_____

_____

_____

リンガポルタ連動テキストをご購入の学生さんは、「リンガポルタ」を無料でご利用いただけます！

本テキストで学習していただく内容に準拠した問題を、オンライン学習システム「リンガポルタ」で学習していただくことができます。PCだけでなく、スマートフォンやタブレットでも学習できます。単語や文法、リスニング力などをよりしっかり身に付けていただくため、ぜひ積極的に活用してください。

リンガポルタの利用にはアカウントとアクセスコードの登録が必要です。登録方法については下記ページにアクセスしてください。

https://www.seibido.co.jp/linguaporta/register.html

本テキスト「Live Escalate Book 3: Summit」のアクセスコードは下記です。

7243-2046-1231-0365-0003-006f-SLL7-W7Q8

・リンガポルタの学習機能（画像はサンプルです。また、すべてのテキストに以下の4つの機能が用意されているわけではありません）

多肢選択

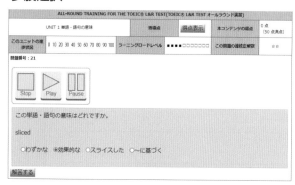

空所補充（音声を使っての聞き取り問題も可能）

単語並びかえ（マウスや手で単語を移動）

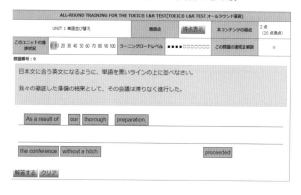

マッチング（マウスや手で単語を移動）

Web動画のご案内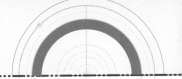

本テキストの映像は、オンラインでのストリーミング再生になります。下記URLよりご利用ください。なお**有効期限は、はじめてログインした時点から1年半**です。

http://st.seibido.co.jp

①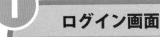

テキストに添付されているシールをはがして、12桁のアクセスコードをご入力ください。

同意してログイン

以下の「利用規約」をご確認頂き、同意する場合は上記ボタン【同意してログイン】を押してください。

利用規約

1. このウェブサイト（以下「本サイト」といいます）は、株式会社成美堂（以下「弊社」といいます）が運営しています。弊社の商品・サービス（以下「本サービス」といいます）利用時の会員登録の有無を問わず、本サイトの利用にあたっては、以下のご利用条件をお読み頂き、これらの条件にご同意の上ご利用ください。

2. 本サービスに関して個別に利用規約がある場合、本規約に加えそれらも適用されます。

3. 本サイトを通じて、弊社の商品を販売する第三者のウェブサイトにご案内ないしリンクされることがあります。リンク先ウェブサイトにおいて提供された個人情報は

巻末に添付されているシールをはがして、アクセスコードをご入力ください。

② メニュー画面

AFP World Focus
−Environment, Health, and Technology−

アクセスコード有効期限：2018年4月30日

🎬 **Video** | 🎵 **Audio**

Lesson 1: Global Warming and Climat... >
Lesson 2: Diet and Health for Long ... >
Lesson 3: Self-Driving for the Futu... >
Lesson 4: Sustaining Biodiversity a... >
Lesson 5: 3D Printers for Creating ... >
Lesson 6: IT and Education >
Lesson 7: Protection from Natural D... >
Lesson 8: Practical Uses of Drones ... >

「Video」または「Audio」を選択すると、それぞれストリーミング再生ができます。

③ 再生画面

AFP World Focus
−Environment, Health, and Technology−

アクセスコード有効期限：2018年4月30日

Lesson 2:
Diet and Health for Long Lives
食習慣：長生きのためのスーパーフードを探す

推奨動作環境

【PC OS】
Windows 7〜 / Mac 10.8〜

【Mobile OS】
iOS / Android ※Androidの場合は4.x〜が推奨

【Desktop ブラウザ】
Internet Explorer 9〜 / Firefox / Chrome / Safari / Microsoft Edge

139

TEXT PRODUCTION STAFF

edited by	編集
Takashi Kudo	工藤 隆志
Hiromi Oota	太田 裕美

cover design by	表紙デザイン
Nobuyoshi Fujino	藤野 伸芳

text design by	本文デザイン
Ruben Frosali	ルーベン・フロサリ

CD PRODUCTION STAFF

recorded by	吹き込み者
Rachel Walzer (AmE)	レイチェル・ワルザー (アメリカ英語)
Howard Colefield (AmE)	ハワード・コールフィルド (アメリカ英語)
Dominic Allen (AmE)	ドミニク・アレン (アメリカ英語)
Karen Haedrich (AmE)	カレン・ヘドリック (アメリカ英語)

Live Escalate Book 3: Summit

2022年1月20日　初版発行
2024年2月25日　第4刷発行

著　　者　角山 照彦
　　　　　Live ABC editors

発 行 者　佐野 英一郎

発 行 所　株式会社 成美堂
　　　　　〒101-0052　東京都千代田区神田小川町3-22
　　　　　TEL 03-3291-2261　FAX 03-3293-5490
　　　　　https://www.seibido.co.jp

印刷・製本　(株)加藤文明社

ISBN 978-4-7919-7243-2　　　　　　　　　　Printed in Japan